GCSE AQA
French

The only way to make sure you're ready for the French exams is to practise.

Luckily, this CGP Workbook has plenty of it — there are exam-style questions to test you on reading, writing, listening <u>and</u> speaking, plus grammar practice to check you know your *passé composé* from your *imparfait*.

You'll also find all the audio you need for the speaking and listening questions, plus model answer videos on CGP RevisionHub. Don't say we never treat you.

Unlock CGP RevisionHub

Just scan a QR code in the book to access the CGP RevisionHub.
Or go to **cgpbooks.co.uk/revise** and enter this code!

1710 9651 5361 9373

By the way, this code only works for one person. If somebody else has used this book before you, they might have already claimed the code.

Exam Practice Workbook
with new *CGP RevisionHub*

Contents

How To Use This Book..1

Section One — General Stuff

Numbers, Times, Days and Dates..2
Questions and Being Polite..4
Opinions..6

Theme 1: People and Lifestyle

Section Two — Identity and Relationships with Others

About Yourself and My Family & Friends..8
Describing People and Relationships..10

Section Three — Healthy Living and Lifestyle

Food and Healthy & Unhealthy Living..12
Illnesses and Treatments..14

Section Four — Education

School Subjects and School Life..16
School Pressures and Difficulties...18

Section Five — Future Study and Work

Education Post–16 and Career Choices...20

Theme 1 — Mixed Practice

Mixed Practice — Foundation..22
Mixed Practice — Both Tiers..25
Mixed Practice — Higher..28

Theme 2: Popular Culture

Section Six — Free-time Activities

Music, Cinema, Theatre and TV..32
Sport, Going Out and Other Hobbies..34

Section Seven — Customs, Festivals and Celebrations

Customs, Festivals and Celebrations..36

Section Eight — Celebrity Culture

Favourite Celebrities & Celebrity Life...38

Theme 2 — Mixed Practice

Mixed Practice — Foundation..40
Mixed Practice — Both Tiers..43
Mixed Practice — Higher..47

Contents

Theme 3: Communication and the World Around Us

Section Nine — Travel and Tourism
Where to Go, Accommodation and Travel 50
What to Do 52

Section Ten — Media and Technology
Technology and The Internet 54
Social Media 56

Section Eleven — Where People Live
Where You Live and The Home 58
The Local Area, Directions and Weather 60

Section Twelve — Environmental and Social Issues
Protecting the Environment & Environmental Problems 62
Social Issues 64

Theme 3 — Mixed Practice
Mixed Practice — Foundation 66
Mixed Practice — Both Tiers 70
Mixed Practice — Higher 72

Grammar

Section Thirteen — Nouns, Articles and Linking Words
Nouns and Articles 76
Pronouns 78
Conjunctions and Prepositions 80

Section Fourteen — Adjectives and Adverbs
Adjectives 82
Adverbs, Quantifiers and Intensifiers 84
Comparatives and Superlatives 86

Section Fifteen — Verbs and Tenses
Present Tense 88
Past Tenses 90
Talking about the Future & The Conditional 92
Reflexives, Negative Forms & Giving Orders 94
–ing Verbs, Impersonal Verbs & the Passive 96

Answers 98
Listening Transcripts 111
Speaking Transcripts 115

Published by CGP

Editors:
Nathan Mair
Ilana Pearce
Anna Stringer
Alex Thompson

With thanks to Marie-Laure Delvallée, Robbie Driscoll, Emma Duffee,
Natalie Pomier, Véronique Robine and Hannah Roscoe for the proofreading.
With thanks to Alice Dent for the copyright research.

Acknowledgements:
Audio produced by Voice Talent Online.

AQA material is reproduced by permission of AQA.

The worked solutions to questions and commentaries on questions and possible answers in this book have neither been provided by nor approved by AQA.

ISBN: 978 1 83774 195 3
Printed by Elanders Ltd, Newcastle upon Tyne.
Clipart from Corel®

Based on the classic CGP style created by Richard Parsons.

Text, design, layout and original illustrations © Coordination Group Publications Ltd. (CGP) 2025
All rights reserved.

Photocopying this book is not permitted, even if you have a CLA licence.
Extra copies are available from CGP with next day delivery • 0800 1712 712 • www.cgpbooks.co.uk

How To Use This Book

"Why do I need to know how to use this book?" I hear you ask. "I know how to use books. I'm not three." Well, perhaps not. But this is no ordinary book. This book is special...

This book follows the AQA specification

1) The content for AQA GCSE French is divided into **nine topics**. Each topic falls under one of **three themes**:

   | People and lifestyle | Popular culture | Communication and the world around us |

2) In this book, there is usually **one** section for each topic. However, some topics have been **split into two sections** to make things more manageable. There's also a section of **mixed practice** at the end of each theme.

3) Section One covers **'General Stuff'**, with content that's useful across the course.

4) There are also three **grammar sections** that cover the grammar you need to know.

You can sit Higher or Foundation tier

1) You can choose to sit the **Higher-tier exams** or the **Foundation-tier exams**. You have to do the **same** tier for all four French exams. Here are the main **differences** between them:

   - In **Foundation tier**, there's **less vocabulary** and **less grammar** to learn and the questions are slightly easier. In this tier, you can earn up to **Grade 5**.
   - In **Higher tier**, you can achieve **Grades 4-9**, but you'll need to learn **more vocab** and **more complex grammar**.
   - Speak to your **teacher** if you're not sure **which tier** you're sitting.

   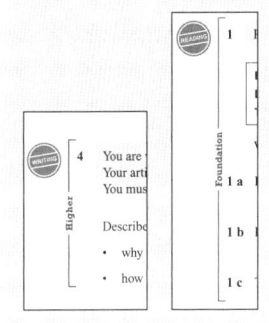

2) In this book, questions that are specific to one of the tiers have been marked up with a **bracket**, like this:

The CGP RevisionHub is full of resources

Scan this QR code to access the CGP RevisionHub, or go to www.cgpbooks.co.uk/cafe

- You can use the online resources on the CGP RevisionHub **alongside this book** as you're revising.
- The RevisionHub contains all the **audio** you'll need for the **listening questions**, and **speaking tracks** so you can hear the teacher part for all the speaking questions in the book.
- There are printable versions of the **transcripts** and speaking and writing **mark schemes** as well.
- It's also got **worked answer videos** for some of the questions, so you can feel more confident about how to answer them.

Time to turn over the page...

No, not like that. Anyway, make the most of the RevisionHub videos in this book. I've put a lot of time and effort into making them perfect, so please don't let my blood, sweat and (actual) tears be in vain...

Find the CGP RevisionHub at cgpbooks.co.uk/cafe

Section One — General Stuff

Numbers, Times, Days and Dates

1 You are talking to your penfriend Nathan on the phone about his weekend. Answer the questions in **English**.

1 a How many bags did Nathan buy?

.... *[1 mark]*

1 b How many letters did he send?

.... *[1 mark]*

1 c How much did his shopping cost in total?

.... *[1 mark]*

1 d How old did Nathan's best friend turn on Saturday?

.... *[1 mark]*

1 e How many presents did his best friend receive?

.... *[1 mark]*

2 Read what these people have written in a forum about their free time, then answer the questions below. Write the correct letters in the boxes.

> Je fais beaucoup de sport pour garder la forme. Le mardi soir, je fais de la natation. Ça commence à dix-sept heures. — **Ana**
>
> Moi, j'aime la musique. Dimanche prochain, avec mon groupe, nous nous préparerons pour un grand concert que nous donnerons le dix-huit août. — **Dorian**
>
> Je passe la plupart de mon temps à lire. Aujourd'hui, j'ai ajouté quatorze livres à ma liste de livres à acheter. Je lis environ quarante livres par an. — **Camille**

2 a Ana goes swimming...

A	on Saturday mornings.
B	on Tuesday evenings.
C	at seven o'clock.

[1 mark]

2 b Dorian's concert will take place...

A	on the 8th April.
B	next Sunday.
C	on the 18th August.

[1 mark]

2 c Camille says she...

A	reads fourteen books each month.
B	buys around forty books each year.
C	spends most of her time reading.

[1 mark]

3 You see some headlines on a French news website.

A	Grève des transports ce samedi
B	L'année scolaire commence le trois septembre
C	Ce samedi soir au cinéma : un nouveau film d'action
D	Conduire en hiver : des informations essentielles
E	Le nouvel hôpital va coûter vingt-deux millions d'euros

Which headline matches each topic? Write the correct letter in each box.

3 a Weather

[1 mark]

3 b School

[1 mark]

3 c Building project

[1 mark]

4 You will hear 4 short sentences. Listen carefully and, using your knowledge of French sounds, write down in **French** exactly what you hear for each sentence.

You will hear each sentence **three** times: the first time as a full sentence, the second time in short sections and the third time again as a full sentence.

Use your knowledge of French sounds and grammar to make sure that what you have written makes sense. Check carefully that your spelling is accurate.

4 a Sentence 1

.... *[2 marks]*

4 b Sentence 2

.... *[2 marks]*

4 c Sentence 3

.... *[2 marks]*

4 d Sentence 4

....

.... *[2 marks]*

Score:

Questions and Being Polite

1 Read these emails sent to a clothing company's customer services department.

> **Eva**: Est-ce que vous avez le pantalon dans une plus grande taille ?
> **Luis**: Est-ce que vous vendez vos produits en ligne ?
> **Toni**: Est-ce qu'il y a une réduction pour les étudiants ?

What is each question about? Write the correct letter in the box.

A	Student discount
B	Returns
C	Clothes sizes
D	Online shop
E	Delivery cost

1 a Eva   ☐ *[1 mark]*

1 b Luis   ☐ *[1 mark]*

1 c Toni   ☐ *[1 mark]*

---

2 You will hear 4 short sentences. Listen carefully and, using your knowledge of French sounds, write down in **French** exactly what you hear for each sentence.

You will hear each sentence **three** times: the first time as a full sentence, the second time in short sections and the third time again as a full sentence.

Use your knowledge of French sounds and grammar to make sure that what you have written makes sense. Check carefully that your spelling is accurate.

2 a Sentence 1

....

.... *[2 marks]*

2 b Sentence 2

....

.... *[2 marks]*

2 c Sentence 3

....

.... *[2 marks]*

2 d Sentence 4

....

.... *[2 marks]*

Section One — General Stuff

3 Using your knowledge of grammar, complete the following sentences in **French**. Choose the correct French word from the three options in the grid. Write the correct **word** in the space.

3 a Est-ce que nous .... du pain ?

| ont | as | avons |

[1 mark]

3 b Quand viens-..................... à la gare ?

| il | tu | on |

[1 mark]

3 c Elle est .... pour ses actions.

| desolé | désolée | désolés |

[1 mark]

4 Translate the following sentences into **French**.

4 a Why do you arrive late on Thursdays?

....

.... *[2 marks]*

4 b Where does the history teacher go for his holidays?

....

.... *[2 marks]*

4 c How much do these fresh vegetables cost?

....

.... *[2 marks]*

4 d Do you like swimming in mountain lakes?

....

.... *[2 marks]*

Opinions

1 These French students are sharing their opinions.

> **Thomas:** J'aime aller à l'école. Cependant, je déteste les cours de sport.
> **Maria:** Selon moi, les vacances à la montagne ne sont pas très agréables car il fait toujours mauvais.
> **Léa:** Ma mère est fière de ses repas — ils sont géniaux.
> **Mehdi:** Je crois que la natation a amélioré ma santé.

Are the opinions of these students positive or negative?

Write **P** for a **positive** opinion

N for a **negative** opinion

P + N for a **positive** and **negative** opinion.

Write the correct letter in each box.

1 a Thomas [ ] *[1 mark]*

1 b Maria [ ] *[1 mark]*

1 c Léa [ ] *[1 mark]*

1 d Mehdi [ ] *[1 mark]*

2 While on a bus in Paris, you overhear two people talking about a singer. Complete the sentences in **English**.

2 a Sabrina is Léa's...

.... *[1 mark]*

2 b Rachid is not interested in Sabrina because he thinks that...

.... *[1 mark]*

2 c Léa says Sabrina's shows are always...

.... *[1 mark]*

2 d Rachid thinks that the main goal of all celebrities is to...

.... *[1 mark]*

3 You are emailing your French penfriend about your likes and dislikes.
Write approximately **90** words in **French**.
You must write something about each bullet point.

Describe:

- what you like to do in the evenings
- your opinion on the last TV programme you watched
- what hobby you will take up next and why.

[15 marks]

4 Read Ana's article about local restaurants.

> «Chez Fatima» est un restaurant espagnol au centre-ville. Le chef vient de Madrid, même si les serveurs sont tous français. J'adore sa nourriture, mais je ne recommande pas ce restaurant car il n'y a jamais de tables libres. Par contre, je préfère «Le Café des Amis», un café près de chez moi, car il propose un super petit-déjeuner anglais, même si, selon moi, c'est un peu cher. Je le prends toujours avec **une tasse** de thé.

Complete these sentences. Write the letter for the correct option in each box.

4 a 'Chez Fatima' serves...

A	Spanish food.
B	English food.
C	French food.

[1 mark]

4 b Ana doesn't recommend it because...

A	the waiters are French.
B	it's always full.
C	it doesn't serve breakfast.

[1 mark]

4 c Ana prefers 'Le Café des Amis' because...

A	it does a good breakfast.
B	it's near her house.
C	it's cheap.

[1 mark]

4 d Read the final sentence again. What does '**une tasse**' mean?

A	a box
B	a cup
C	a spoon

[1 mark]

Score:

About Yourself and My Family & Friends

1 Your friend has sent you a photo of their family. What is in this photo? Write **three** sentences in **French**.

1 a .... *[2 marks]*

1 b .... *[2 marks]*

1 c .... *[2 marks]*

2 Translate the following sentences into **English**.

2 a Je suis née en Angleterre, mais ma famille est allemande.

....

.... *[2 marks]*

2 b Il parle français et espagnol.

....

.... *[2 marks]*

2 c J'ai un père, une belle-mère et beaucoup de frères et sœurs.

....

.... *[2 marks]*

2 d J'adore passer du temps avec mes cousins. Nous chattons souvent.

....

.... *[2 marks]*

2 e Elle ne s'entend pas bien avec sa tante et son oncle.

....

.... *[2 marks]*

3 A French exchange student is coming to stay with you.
Write a short description of your life for them.
Write approximately **50** words in **French**.
You must write something about each bullet point.

Mention:
- your age
- where you live
- your parents
- your siblings
- what your friends are like.

[10 marks]

4 You will hear 4 short sentences. Listen carefully and, using your knowledge of French sounds, write down in **French** exactly what you hear for each sentence.

You will hear each sentence **three** times: the first time as a full sentence, the second time in short sections and the third time again as a full sentence.

Use your knowledge of French sounds and grammar to make sure that what you have written makes sense. Check carefully that your spelling is accurate.

4 a Sentence 1

....

.... *[2 marks]*

4 b Sentence 2

....

.... *[2 marks]*

4 c Sentence 3

....

.... *[2 marks]*

4 d Sentence 4

....

.... *[2 marks]*

Score:

Describing People and Relationships

1 Translate the following sentences into **French**.

1 a My brother's child looks like our father.

....

.... *[2 marks]*

1 b They are very proud to be hard-working.

....

.... *[2 marks]*

1 c The man and the woman argue a lot.

....

.... *[2 marks]*

1 d Communication and trust are very important.

....

.... *[2 marks]*

1 e My uncle used to be single.

....

.... *[2 marks]*

2 You are writing an email to your friend about a recent wedding in your family.
Write approximately **90** words in **French**.
You must write something about each bullet point.

Describe:

- what happened at the wedding
- your opinion on marriage
- whether you will get married in future.

[15 marks]

Section Two — Identity and Relationships with Others

3 You read this page of a dating website. Answer the questions below in **English**.

> Je m'appelle Sabrina. Je viens de Nantes, mais j'habite à Lille avec ma petite sœur, Clara. Je suis drôle et mes amis disent que je suis très sensible. J'ai besoin d'un homme gentil et patient, parce que mon dernier copain m'a trompée. J'aimerais rencontrer quelqu'un qui ne fume pas, parce que je déteste les cigarettes. Je suis aussi sportive, donc mon partenaire idéal ne devrait pas être paresseux. J'adore regarder les oiseaux donc ça serait super s'il visitait des parcs nationaux avec moi. J'espère vous rencontrer bientôt !

3 a What word do Sabrina's friends use to describe her?

.... *[1 mark]*

3 b Why does Sabrina want a partner who is kind and patient?

.... *[1 mark]*

3 c What are **two** traits that Sabrina's ideal partner would **not** have?

1. ....

2. .... *[2 marks]*

3 d Where would Sabrina like to go with her new partner?

.... *[1 mark]*

---

4 You hear this radio show about marriage. Answer the questions in **English**.

4 a Why does Sylvie want to stay single?

.... *[1 mark]*

4 b Why does Richard say he isn't married yet?

.... *[1 mark]*

Section Three — Healthy Living and Lifestyle

Food and Healthy & Unhealthy Living

1 In France, you hear this radio phone-in programme about healthy living. Choose the correct topic for each caller and write the letter in the box.

A	exercise
B	losing weight
C	healthy eating
D	sleep
E	relaxation

1 a ☐ *[1 mark]*

1 b ☐ *[1 mark]*

H 1 c ☐ *[1 mark]*

2 Spend a few minutes looking at the two photos.
Make notes on them to use during the test.

Your teacher will ask you to talk about the content of the photos. You should talk for approximately **one and a half minutes**. **You must say at least one thing about each photo.**

After you have spoken about the content of the photos, your teacher will then ask you questions related to **any** of the topics within the theme of **People and lifestyle**.

Scan the QR code to hear the teacher part of the question, or you can find the transcript in the back of the book.

[25 marks]

3 Translate the following sentences into **English**.

3 a Je pense qu'il est assez actif.

....

.... *[2 marks]*

3 b Ma mère ne boit pas d'alcool et ne fume pas.

....

.... *[2 marks]*

3 c Normalement, je fais beaucoup de sport pour rester en forme.

....

.... *[2 marks]*

3 d Je vais aller à la piscine demain.

....

.... *[2 marks]*

3 e Hier soir, j'ai préparé un repas équilibré pour ma famille.

....

.... *[2 marks]*

4 You are writing an article encouraging teenagers to avoid drinking, smoking and drugs. Your article is for a local magazine. Write approximately **150** words in **French**. You must write something about both bullet points.

Describe:

- why drinking, smoking and drugs are bad for you
- how we can encourage people to avoid them. *[25 marks]*

Score:

Illnesses and Treatments

1 Using your knowledge of grammar, complete the following sentences in **French**.
Choose the correct French word from the options in the grid.
Write the correct **word** in the space.

1 a Je dois .... soin de ma santé.

| pris | prends | prendre |

[1 mark]

1 b Je suis .... malade.

| tomber | tombé | tombes |

[1 mark]

1 c Ma mère a mal .... tête.

| à la | au | aux |

[1 mark]

2 You read Théo's blog post about an upcoming football match.

> Demain, il y aura un match important pour mon équipe de football. Cependant, je m'inquiète parce que les joueurs ont eu beaucoup de problèmes de santé. Chloé s'est cassé le bras et donc elle ne sera pas disponible pour le match. Zoé a mal à l'oreille et donc je lui ai conseillé d'aller chez le médecin et de ne pas jouer demain.

Complete these sentences. Write the letter for the correct option in each box.

2 a Théo feels...

A	excited about the football match.
B	worried about the football match.
C	disappointed about the football match.

[1 mark]

2 b Chloé can't play because she has...

A	broken her arm.
B	injured her back.
C	got a sore ear.

[1 mark]

2 c Théo told Zoé to...

A	take Chloé's place in the team.
B	visit the doctor.
C	get some advice.

[1 mark]

3 You read this letter in the local newspaper. Answer the questions below in **English**.

> Je m'appelle Mathis. Récemment, j'ai eu un accident de voiture. J'ai eu très peur, mais ce n'était pas grave. Après l'accident, je suis allé à l'hôpital pour recevoir des soins médicaux. La médecin m'a dit de rester chez moi pendant deux semaines et d'éviter les activités sportives. Malheureusement, j'ai mal aux mains et au dos.

3 a What was Mathis involved in recently?

.... *[1 mark]*

3 b Give one thing the doctor advised Mathis to do.

.... *[1 mark]*

3 c What **two** body parts are causing Mathis pain?

1. ....

2. .... *[2 marks]*

---

4 You will hear 4 short sentences. Listen carefully and, using your knowledge of French sounds, write down in **French** exactly what you hear for each sentence.

You will hear each sentence **three** times: the first time as a full sentence, the second time in short sections and the third time again as a full sentence.

Use your knowledge of French sounds and grammar to make sure that what you have written makes sense. Check carefully that your spelling is accurate.

4 a Sentence 1

.... *[2 marks]*

4 b Sentence 2

.... *[2 marks]*

4 c Sentence 3

.... *[2 marks]*

4 d Sentence 4

.... *[2 marks]*

Score:

Section Three — Healthy Living and Lifestyle

Section Four — Education

School Subjects and School Life

1 When your teacher asks you, read aloud the following text **in French**.

> Je prends le bus pour aller au collège.
>
> La journée commence tôt.
>
> Mon premier cours, c'est histoire.
>
> La technologie est ma matière préférée.
>
> Pendant la récré, je parle avec mes amis.

- You will then be asked four questions **in French** that relate to the topic of **Education and work**.

- In order to score the highest marks, **answer all four questions as fully as you can**.

[15 marks]

Foundation

2 During a school exchange, you hear these young people talking about their studies. Write the correct letters in the boxes to complete the sentences.

2 a Inès thinks that...

A	languages are not easy.
B	physics is the hardest science.
C	it's useful to speak another language.

[1 mark]

2 b Yasmina thinks it's essential to...

A	talk to others.
B	not waste your time in front of a screen.
C	know how to use a computer.

[1 mark]

2 c Mehdi thinks that...

A	young people use computers too much.
B	we should use computers for everything.
C	computers help you to study maths.

[1 mark]

3 You read an internet forum about school.

> **Dorian:** Mon école a beaucoup d'espace, mais certains profs ne sont pas très intéressants.
>
> **Fatima:** Les cours de science sont très pratiques et nous apprenons beaucoup sur le monde.
>
> **Théo:** Il faut faire les cours de sport dehors, même dans le froid. C'est une torture !
>
> **Emma:** Le collège ne propose pas de cours de musique. Dommage, car à mon avis c'est une matière essentielle.
>
> **Lucie:** Il y a beaucoup de choix à la bibliothèque, mais on ne peut pas dire la même chose de la cuisine. Je suis végétarienne, et je dois toujours prendre le même déjeuner.

What do these people think about their school?

Write **P** for a **positive** opinion
N for a **negative** opinion
P + N for a **positive** and **negative** opinion.

Write the correct letter in each box.

3 a Dorian ☐ *[1 mark]*

3 b Fatima ☐ *[1 mark]*

3 c Théo ☐ *[1 mark]*

3 d Emma ☐ *[1 mark]*

3 e Lucie ☐ *[1 mark]*

4 You are writing an email to your French pen friend about your school.
Write approximately **90** words in **French**.
You must write something about each bullet point.

Describe:

- what you like and dislike about your school
- a lesson you found interesting recently
- what you will do next week at school.

[15 marks]

Score: ☐

Section Four — Education

School Pressures and Difficulties

1 These young people are talking about school challenges. Which **two** challenges does each student mention? Write the correct letters in the boxes.

A	Exams
B	Homework
C	Peer pressure
D	Student behaviour
E	School rules

1 a ☐ ☐ *[2 marks]*

1 b ☐ ☐ *[2 marks]*

2 Translate the following sentences into **English**.

2 a Le collège nous oblige à porter un uniforme scolaire.

....

.... *[2 marks]*

2 b Selon moi, le comportement est le plus grand problème à l'école.

....

.... *[2 marks]*

2 c Malheureusement, je me suis trompé dans le contrôle d'anglais.

....

.... *[2 marks]*

2 d Le professeur corrigera mes devoirs pendant la récréation.

....

.... *[2 marks]*

2 e La directrice ne permet pas aux élèves d'utiliser leurs portables.

....

.... *[2 marks]*

3 You are writing a report. Your report is about problems at your school. Write about **150** words in **French**.
You must write something about both bullet points.

Describe:
- what problems you have faced at school
- how the school will solve these problems in the future.

[25 marks]

4 Translate the following sentences into **French**.

4 a I am worried for the geography exam on Tuesday.

....

.... [2 marks]

4 b My friend's grades are always great.

....

.... [2 marks]

4 c I think that the rules at college are quite strict.

....

.... [2 marks]

4 d Wearing green trousers to school is prohibited.

....

.... [2 marks]

4 e Often, I help the other students with their homework.

....

.... [2 marks]

Score:

Section Five — Future Study and Work

Education Post-16 and Career Choices

1 You read Ana's message about future options. Answer the questions below **in English**.

> L'année dernière, j'ai essayé d'aller à l'université. Cependant, ma prof m'a dit que je n'étais pas prête. J'ai trouvé un apprentissage pour améliorer mes compétences pratiques et gagner de l'argent.

1 a What did Ana try to do last year?

.... *[1 mark]*

1 b Why did Ana change her plans?

.... *[1 mark]*

1 c What **two** reasons does Ana give for finding an apprenticeship?

1. ....

2. .... *[2 marks]*

2 These French people are talking about their jobs.
What jobs do they do? Write the correct letter in each box.

2 a Marie ☐   *[1 mark]*

2 b Enzo ☐   *[1 mark]*

2 c Dorian ☐   *[1 mark]*

2 d Fathia ☐   *[1 mark]*

A	Police officer
B	Waiter
C	Singer
D	Headteacher
E	Carer

3 You are writing a letter to your Togolese friend about future career options.
Write approximately **90** words in **French**.
You must write something about each bullet point.

Describe:

- what jobs people in your family do
- what you wanted to be when you were little
- your plans for the future.

[15 marks]

4 Read these internet posts about further education.

Yanis	Pour certains emplois, c'est mieux de faire un apprentissage. Quand on fait un apprentissage, on apprend un métier et on gagne de l'expérience.
Sarah	Si on veut une carrière intéressante, on doit continuer son éducation. Moi, je veux réussir mon bac et après ça, je vais décider quoi faire.
Manon	C'est très important de réussir aux examens. Je vais continuer à étudier parce que je sais ce que je veux faire plus tard et j'ai besoin du bac.
Nadia	Je pense qu'on peut étudier et travailler en même temps. Moi, je vais au collège pendant la journée et je suis serveuse dans un restaurant le soir.

Match the correct person with each of the following questions. Write **Y** for **Yanis**, **S** for **Sarah**, **M** for **Manon** or **N** for **Nadia**. Write the correct letter in each box.

4 a Who needs qualifications to get the job they want? *[1 mark]*

4 b Who thinks it's a good idea to have a job while studying? *[1 mark]*

4 c Who will make plans after doing A-levels? *[1 mark]*

4 d Who wants to learn on the job? *[1 mark]*

5 You are talking to your Moroccan friend. Your teacher will play the part of your friend and will speak first.

- You should address your friend as *tu*.
- When you see this – **?** – you will have to ask a question.

In order to score full marks, you must include a verb in your response to each task.

1. Describe your dream job. (Give **one** detail.)
2. Say whether you would like to go to university and why. (Give **one** opinion and **one** reason.)
? 3. Ask your friend about their career plans.
4. Say what you would like to do on a gap year. (Give **two** details.)
5. Give one subject that you study and explain why you decided to study it. (Give **one** detail and **one** reason.)

[10 marks]

Score:

Mixed Practice — Foundation

1 A pupil is studying in a classroom.
What is in this photo?
Write **five** sentences in **French**.

1 a .... *[2 marks]*

1 b .... *[2 marks]*

1 c .... *[2 marks]*

1 d .... *[2 marks]*

1 e .... *[2 marks]*

2 Using your knowledge of grammar, complete the following sentences in **French**.
Choose the correct French word from the three options in the grid.
Write the correct **word** in the space.

2 a Cette maison est ....

| affreux | affreuses | affreuse |

[1 mark]

2 b J'ai .... un gâteau.

| apporte | apporté | apportez |

[1 mark]

2 c Nous voulons savoir .... vérité.

| la | le | les |

[1 mark]

2 d Elles .... plus intelligentes.

| devenir | deviennent | devient |

[1 mark]

2 e Les garçons sont ....

| heureuses | heureuse | heureux |

[1 mark]

3 When your teacher asks you, read aloud the following text **in French**.

> Aujourd'hui, elle visite l'université avec ses amis.
>
> Les bâtiments historiques sont beaux.
>
> Les professeurs sont géniaux et les étudiants sont très gentils.
>
> L'année scolaire commence le neuf septembre.
>
> Elle va étudier pour réussir au concours.

- You will then be asked four questions **in French** that relate to the topic of **Education and work**.
- In order to score the highest marks, **answer all four questions as fully as you can**.

[15 marks]

4 Translate the following sentences into **English**.

4 a Après l'accident, j'avais mal à la tête.

....

.... *[2 marks]*

4 b Ma mère est tombée hier.

....

.... *[2 marks]*

4 c Demain, je vais organiser une réunion.

....

.... *[2 marks]*

4 d Il y a une urgence médicale à l'hôpital.

....

.... *[2 marks]*

4 e La médecin trouve toujours une solution au problème.

....

.... *[2 marks]*

5 You hear some French students talking about their school life. What is the opinion of the students on the following aspects?

Write **P** for a **positive** opinion

N for a **negative** opinion

P + N for a **positive** and **negative** opinion.

5 a Teachers

[1 mark]

5 b Exams

[1 mark]

5 c Facilities

[1 mark]

5 d Other students

[1 mark]

6 Translate the following sentences into **French**.

6 a I have a sister.

....

.... [2 marks]

6 b She gets on well with our parents.

....

.... [2 marks]

6 c There are a lot of different generations in my family.

....

.... [2 marks]

6 d Last year, I met my partner at a party.

....

.... [2 marks]

6 e I hope to get married one day.

....

.... [2 marks]

Score:

Theme 1 — Mixed Practice

Mixed Practice — Both Tiers

1 Listen to these job adverts and choose the two correct statements for each one. Write the correct letters in the boxes.

1 a

A	This is a sociable job.
B	This is a physical job.
C	Knowing how to ride a bike is essential.
D	You will need to take care of animals.

☐ ☐ *[2 marks]*

1 b

A	People of any age are encouraged to apply.
B	Being able to drive is important.
C	It's a summer job.
D	The ability to work with others is essential.

☐ ☐ *[2 marks]*

1 c (Higher)

A	For this job, you need qualifications.
B	You have to have a sense of humour.
C	You have to work every day of the week.
D	It's a job that is useful for the future.
E	The work is always easy.

☐ ☐ *[2 marks]*

2 These young people are talking about themselves.

> **Mathis**: Je suis bisexuel et mon meilleur ami est hétéro.
> **Lola**: Je suis suisse et mon identité est importante pour moi.
> **Camille**: J'ai les yeux verts et les cheveux bruns et courts.

In each box, write **M** for **Mathis**, **L** for **Lola** or **C** for **Camille**.

2 a Who talks about their best friend? ☐ *[1 mark]*

2 b Who talks about their appearance? ☐ *[1 mark]*

2 c Who says they are European? ☐ *[1 mark]*

2 d Who talks about sexuality? ☐ *[1 mark]*

2 e Who says that their identity means a lot to them? ☐ *[1 mark]*

3 You will hear 4 short sentences. Listen carefully and, using your knowledge of French sounds, write down in **French** exactly what you hear for each sentence.

You will hear each sentence **three** times: the first time as a full sentence, the second time in short sections and the third time again as a full sentence.

Use your knowledge of French sounds and grammar to make sure that what you have written makes sense. Check carefully that your spelling is accurate.

Foundation

3 a Sentence 1

....

.... *[2 marks]*

3 b Sentence 2

....

.... *[2 marks]*

3 c Sentence 3

....

.... *[2 marks]*

Higher

3 d Sentence 4

....

.... *[2 marks]*

4 You are writing an article about how you stay healthy.
Write approximately **90** words in **French**.
You must write something about each bullet point.

Describe:

- which bad habits you avoid
- a healthy meal that you ate recently
- what exercise you will do next week. *[15 marks]*

Theme 1 — Mixed Practice

5 You hear some French students talking about healthcare. What is their opinion on the following aspects?

Write **P** for a **positive** opinion

N for a **negative** opinion

P + N for a **positive** and **negative** opinion.

5 a Appointments

[1 mark]

5 b Doctors

[1 mark]

5 c Staff

[1 mark]

5 d Waiting times

[1 mark]

6 Some young people were interviewed as part of an anti-smoking campaign. Listen to the interview and complete the sentences in **English**.

6 a Myriam thinks that smoking is...

....

She hates other people smoking because...

.... *[2 marks]*

6 b Jules says that smoking helps him to...

....

His girlfriend thinks he should try to...

.... *[2 marks]*

6 c Fatima used to smoke but...

....

She realised that...

.... *[2 marks]*

Score:

Mixed Practice — Higher

 1   You will hear 4 short sentences. Listen carefully and, using your knowledge of French sounds, write down in **French** exactly what you hear for each sentence.

You will hear each sentence **three** times: the first time as a full sentence, the second time in short sections and the third time again as a full sentence.

Use your knowledge of French sounds and grammar to make sure that what you have written makes sense. Check carefully that your spelling is accurate.

1 a   Sentence 1

....

.... *[2 marks]*

1 b   Sentence 2

....

.... *[2 marks]*

1 c   Sentence 3

....

.... *[2 marks]*

1 d   Sentence 4

....

.... *[2 marks]*

 2   You are writing an article for a lifestyle magazine.
Your article is about getting on with your family.
Write about **150** words in **French**.
You must write something about both bullet points.

Describe:

- your relationship with your family
- a conflict you had with a family member recently. *[25 marks]*

3   Spend a few minutes looking at the two photos.
    Make notes on them to use during the test.

    Your teacher will ask you to talk about the content of the photos.
    You should talk for approximately **one and a half minutes**.
    You must say at least one thing about each photo.

    After you have spoken about the content of the photos, your teacher will
    then ask you questions related to **any** of the topics within the theme of
    People and lifestyle.

[25 marks]

4   You read Alessandro's blog about his school experience.

> *Quand je suis entré en troisième, la musique est rapidement devenue ma matière préférée parce que les cours étaient formidables. La prof m'a vraiment inspiré, donc je jouais souvent du piano. Cependant, les autres profs nous ont toujours donné des contrôles. Je détestais ça. Je m'inquiétais aussi parce que les autres élèves étaient méchants.*

Answer the questions in **English**.

4 a   When did music become Alessandro's favourite subject?

    .... *[1 mark]*

4 b   What made Alessandro practise piano so often?

    .... *[1 mark]*

4 c   What are **two** things that Alessandro did **not** like about school?

    1. ....

    2. .... *[2 marks]*

5 When your teacher asks you, read aloud the following text **in French**.

> Selon les conseils des experts, garder la forme est essentiel.
>
> Les médecins ont longtemps prévenu le public contre les risques du tabac.
>
> Il faut aussi bouger souvent et bien manger.
>
> Si on se blesse, on doit aller à l'hôpital.
>
> Il y a des traitements là-bas qui peuvent sauver des vies.

- You will then be asked four questions **in French** that relate to the topic of **Healthy living and lifestyle**.
- In order to score the highest marks, **answer all four questions as fully as you can**.

[15 marks]

6 Translate the following sentences into **English**.

6 a Hier, ma prof m'a conseillé de réfléchir à ma future carrière.

....

.... *[2 marks]*

6 b Je vais prendre une année sabbatique avant de m'inscrire à l'université.

....

.... *[2 marks]*

6 c À l'avenir, elle veut être chercheuse ou scientifique.

....

.... *[2 marks]*

6 d Le développement du commerce est très important pour l'économie.

....

.... *[2 marks]*

6 e Selon une enquête, la plupart des jeunes ne peuvent pas trouver un emploi.

....

.... *[2 marks]*

Theme 1 — Mixed Practice

7 You are writing an article for an educational blog.
Your article is about school work.
Write about **150** words in **French**.
You must write something about both bullet points.

Describe:

- the positive aspects of homework
- how you will prepare for your exams.

[25 marks]

8 You are talking to your French friend. Your teacher will play the part of your friend and will speak first.

- You should address your friend as *tu*.
- When you see this – ? – you will have to ask a question.

> **In order to score full marks, you must include a verb in your response to each task.**
>
> 1. Describe the personality of one of your friends. (Give **one** detail.)
> 2. Say what someone in your family looks like. (Give **one** detail.)
> ? 3. Ask your friend about their siblings.
> 4. Say if you would like to have children in the future and why / why not. (Give **one** opinion and **one** reason.)
> 5. Talk about an activity you recently did with your family. (Give **two** details.)

[10 marks]

9 While in a café in Canada, you overhear two people talking about their jobs. Complete the sentences in **English**.

9 a Morgane says that she wants...

.... *[1 mark]*

9 b Zoé suggests that Morgane should...

.... *[1 mark]*

9 c Morgane would rather...

.... *[1 mark]*

9 d For a long time, Morgane has been interested in...

.... *[1 mark]*

Score:

Find the CGP RevisionHub at cgpbooks.co.uk/cafe

Theme 1 — Mixed Practice

Section Six — Free-time Activities

Music, Cinema, Theatre and TV

1 Spend a few minutes looking at the two photos. Make notes on them to use during the test.

Scan the QR code to hear the teacher part of the question, or you can find the transcript in the back of the book.

Your teacher will ask you to talk about the content of the photos. You should talk for approximately **one minute**. **You must say at least one thing about each photo.**

After you have spoken about the content of the photos, your teacher will then ask you questions related to **any** of the topics within the theme of **Popular culture**.

[25 marks]

2 Read this e-mail from Mehdi about a film he saw recently. Answer the questions in **English**.

> Samedi soir, je suis allé au cinéma avec mon copain pour voir un nouveau film d'action. Cependant, on est arrivé en retard car on avait la mauvaise heure. Le film était vraiment nul mais on a beaucoup ri parce que les acteurs étaient mauvais.

2 a When did Mehdi see the film?

.... *[1 mark]*

2 b What type of film did Mehdi watch?

.... *[1 mark]*

2 c Why were they late?

.... *[1 mark]*

2 d Why did Mehdi find the film funny?

.... *[1 mark]*

3 You listen to this French radio conversation.
Choose the correct answer and write the letter in each box.

3 a Lucie thought that the new series...

A	could have been better.
B	was astounding.
C	had some terrifying scenes.

[1 mark]

3 b Luis felt that the show...

A	had good special effects.
B	contained too much advertising.
C	is the type of series he normally likes.

[1 mark]

4 Translate the following sentences into **French**.

4 a I watch TV because I think it is exciting.

....

.... [2 marks]

4 b He would like to learn to play an instrument.

....

.... [2 marks]

4 c My sister used to download songs on the internet.

....

.... [2 marks]

4 d They like most music genres, but they do not like popular music.

....

.... [2 marks]

4 e I am interested in the special effects that they use on stage.

....

.... [2 marks]

Score:

Sport, Going Out and Other Hobbies

1 Translate the following sentences into **English**.

1 a J'aime faire du sport et de l'exercice.

....

.... *[2 marks]*

1 b Ma mère est très active.

....

.... *[2 marks]*

1 c Après l'école, je vais aller à la piscine du centre sportif.

....

.... *[2 marks]*

1 d Je vais bientôt participer à une course.

....

.... *[2 marks]*

1 e La natation est bonne pour la santé.

....

.... *[2 marks]*

2 You are writing an email to your friend about your hobbies.
Write approximately **90** words in **French**.
You must write something about each bullet point.

Describe:
- what you like to do in your free time
- what hobbies you did when you were younger
- what activities you would like to try in the future. *[15 marks]*

Section Six — Free-time Activities

3 You hear Léa and Rachid talking about a new restaurant.
Answer the questions in **English**.

3 a What **two** negative things does Rachid mention about the restaurant?

1. ....

2. .... *[2 marks]*

3 b What was the main reason why Rachid disliked the restaurant?

.... *[1 mark]*

3 c Give **two** reasons why Léa didn't like the restaurant.

1. ....

2. .... *[2 marks]*

4 A team is taking part in a football tournament.
What is in this photo?
Write **five** sentences in **French**.

4 a .... *[2 marks]*

4 b .... *[2 marks]*

4 c .... *[2 marks]*

4 d .... *[2 marks]*

4 e .... *[2 marks]*

Score:

Section Six — Free-time Activities

Section Seven — Customs, Festivals and Celebrations

Customs, Festivals and Celebrations

1 You are talking to your Swiss friend. Your teacher will play the part of your friend and will speak first.

- You should address your friend as *tu*.
- When you see this – **?** – you will have to ask a question.

In order to score full marks, you must include a verb in your response to each task.

1. Describe a festival or tradition in your country. (Give **one** detail.)
2. Say how you normally celebrate that festival or tradition. (Give **one** detail.)
3. Describe your favourite festival or tradition. (Give **one** detail.)
? 4. Ask your friend a question about their birthday.
5. Say what you got for your last birthday. (Give **one** detail.)

[10 marks]

2 You overhear Zoé telling her friend about how she celebrated Valentine's Day. Write the correct letters in the boxes to complete the sentences.

2 a Zoé and her girlfriend...

A	watched TV programmes together.
B	had an expensive dinner at a restaurant.
C	went to a music festival.

[1 mark]

2 b She received...

A	a message from her girlfriend.
B	some flowers and a small gift.
C	tickets to see a concert.

[1 mark]

2 c Valentine's Day is special to Zoé because...

A	it gives her the chance to throw a party.
B	she can enjoy the day with her girlfriend.
C	it allows her to express her feelings.

[1 mark]

3 Read Marie's blog post about festivals in Belgium.

> Ici, en Belgique, nous avons aussi une « Fête Nationale », mais ce n'est pas la même qu'en France. On la célèbre le 21 juillet, surtout dans la capitale du pays, en organisant des activités sportives et un grand spectacle.
>
> Cependant, à mon avis, le meilleur événement de l'année est le Festival d'Été, qui dure dix jours. J'adore y aller chaque été avec mes copains. On profite du beau temps — tous les concerts sont dehors et ils sont super. On peut y découvrir de la musique de plus ou moins tous les genres. En plus, on invite des musiciens du monde entier pour participer au festival, donc c'est très international.

Answer the following questions in **English**.

3 a Name **two** events that take place on Belgium's national holiday.

1. ....

2. .... *[2 marks]*

3 b What does Marie think of the Summer Festival? Give **one** detail.

.... *[1 mark]*

3 c What type of music do they play at the festival? Give **one** detail.

.... *[1 mark]*

3 d Where do the musicians playing at the festival come from? Give **one** detail.

.... *[1 mark]*

4 You are writing an email to your French friend about a party you are planning.
Write approximately **90** words in **French**.
You must write something about each bullet point.

Describe:

- what you are celebrating
- how you will celebrate — e.g. what activities you will do
- another party you went to last year. *[15 marks]*

Score:

Section Eight — Celebrity Culture

Favourite Celebrities & Celebrity Life

 1 When your teacher asks you, read aloud the following text **in French**.

> Mon héros était un influenceur qui faisait des vidéos drôles en ligne.
>
> Je pensais qu'il était la voix de notre génération.
>
> Pourtant, j'ai maintenant des doutes sur sa personnalité.
>
> Récemment, son comportement a fait scandale.
>
> Il s'est excusé, mais j'ai beaucoup moins de respecte pour lui.

- You will then be asked four questions **in French** that relate to the topic of **Celebrity Culture**.
- In order to score the highest marks, **answer all four questions as fully as you can**.

[15 marks]

 2 You will hear 4 short sentences. Listen carefully and, using your knowledge of French sounds, write down in **French** exactly what you hear for each sentence.

You will hear each sentence **three** times: the first time as a full sentence, the second time in short sections and the third time again as a full sentence.

Use your knowledge of French sounds and grammar to make sure that what you have written makes sense. Check carefully that your spelling is accurate.

2 a Sentence 1

....

.... *[2 marks]*

2 b Sentence 2

....

.... *[2 marks]*

2 c Sentence 3

....

.... *[2 marks]*

2 d Sentence 4

....

.... *[2 marks]*

3   Read this article about a day in the life of Yasmina, a famous singer.

> Le matin, je bois beaucoup d'eau avant de chanter pendant deux heures. Depuis mon succès au concours l'année dernière, j'essaie d'améliorer ma voix, donc je fais des exercices spéciaux. Ensuite, je me prépare à rencontrer mon équipe.
>
> Nous écrivons les paroles de ma nouvelle chanson, et puis je réponds aux commentaires sur ma dernière vidéo. J'adore ma communauté en ligne parce que les gens qui me suivent sont tous sympas. Je suis fière de les représenter.

Complete these sentences. Write the letter for the correct option in each box.

3 a To improve her voice, Yasmina...

A	drinks water every two hours.
B	takes part in competitions.
C	does vocal exercises.

[1 mark]

3 b Yasmina writes the lyrics to her new song...

A	on her own.
B	with her team.
C	with her online supporters.

[1 mark]

3 c Yasmina finds her followers to be...

A	sympathetic.
B	proud.
C	nice.

[1 mark]

4   You are writing an article about fame. Your article is for an online magazine.
Write approximately **150** words in **French**.
You must write something about both bullet points.

Describe:

- the benefits and drawbacks of being famous

- a celebrity you have met or would like to meet in the future.

[25 marks]

Score:

Mixed Practice — Foundation

1 Spend a few minutes looking at the two photos.
Make notes on them to use during the test.

Your teacher will ask you to talk about the content of the photos.
You should talk for approximately **one minute**.
You must say at least one thing about each photo.

After you have spoken about the content of the photos, your teacher will then ask you questions related to **any** of the topics within the theme of **Popular culture**.

[25 marks]

2 Read these emails sent to a local community centre.

> **Ana**: Est-ce que vous organisez une fête de Noël ?
> **Nathan**: Est-ce que les cours de musique commencent jeudi ?
> **Théo**: Est-ce qu'il y a des concours sportifs ? J'adore jouer au foot.

What is each question about? Write the correct letter in the box.

A	Volunteering
B	Celebrations
C	Sports events
D	Music lessons
E	Membership fees

2 a Ana ☐ *[1 mark]*

2 b Nathan ☐ *[1 mark]*

2 c Théo ☐ *[1 mark]*

3 Translate the following sentences into **English**.

3 a Je fais de la natation le lundi.

....

.... *[2 marks]*

3 b C'est mon rêve d'apprendre à jouer d'un instrument.

....

.... *[2 marks]*

3 c Ce week-end, nous allons aller à un festival.

....

.... *[2 marks]*

3 d Chaque soir, j'écoute ma chanteuse préférée.

....

.... *[2 marks]*

3 e Hier, c'était un jour férié, donc je suis allé à la plage.

....

.... *[2 marks]*

4 When your teacher asks you, read aloud the following text **in French**.

> Je m'intéresse vraiment à la mode.
>
> Les célébrités ont souvent beaucoup de style.
>
> Ma star préférée porte toujours de beaux vêtements.
>
> Je voudrais étudier le théâtre après le collège.
>
> Mon copain n'aime pas voir les pièces — il préfère le sport.

- You will then be asked four questions **in French** that relate to the topic of **Popular culture**.

- In order to score the highest marks, **answer all four questions as fully as you can**.

[15 marks]

5 You see an online forum. Three friends are talking about religious festivals.

Clara	Je suis chrétienne. À Noël, je vais à l'église avec mes parents. Mon frère ne vient pas avec nous car il est bouddhiste, mais il vient chez nous plus tard.
Yanis	Je viens d'une famille juive. Hanoukka est un festival traditionnel qui dure huit jours. On chante des chansons ensemble et on joue à des jeux.
Toni	Le mois dernier, ma mère a participé à une fête musulmane. Moi, je ne m'intéresse pas à la religion.

Match the correct person with each of the following questions.
Write **C** for **Clara**, **Y** for **Yanis** or **T** for **Toni**. Write the correct letter in each box.

5 a Who is Christian? [1 mark]

5 b Who is not religious? [1 mark]

5 c Who celebrates for several days? [1 mark]

5 d Who visits a religious building? [1 mark]

5 e Who mentions a religious festival that happened recently? [1 mark]

6 You hear some French students talking about celebrity life.
What is the opinion of the students on the following aspects?

Write **P** for a **positive** opinion

N for a **negative** opinion

P + N for a **positive** and **negative** opinion.

6 a Friendships [1 mark]

6 b Influence [1 mark]

6 c Media [1 mark]

6 d Money [1 mark]

Score:

Mixed Practice — Both Tiers

 1 You will hear 4 short sentences. Listen carefully and, using your knowledge of French sounds, write down in **French** exactly what you hear for each sentence.

You will hear each sentence **three** times: the first time as a full sentence, the second time in short sections and the third time again as a full sentence.

Use your knowledge of French sounds and grammar to make sure that what you have written makes sense. Check carefully that your spelling is accurate.

1 a Sentence 1

....

.... *[2 marks]*

1 b Sentence 2

....

.... *[2 marks]*

1 c Sentence 3

....

.... *[2 marks]*

1 d Sentence 4

....

.... *[2 marks]*

 2 You are writing an email to your friend about sport.
Write approximately **90** words in **French**.
You must write something about each bullet point.

Describe:

- what your favourite sports are
- what exercise you have done this week
- a sporting event you would like to go to. *[15 marks]*

3 Translate the following sentences into **French**.

3 a I don't like to watch television. I prefer to go to the theatre.

....

.... *[2 marks]*

3 b There are lots of famous actors in this new action film.

....

.... *[2 marks]*

3 c I like international politics so I read newspapers.

....

.... *[2 marks]*

3 d My favourite author has written a new book.

....

.... *[2 marks]*

4 You listen to this podcast episode. Mehdi is talking about Eid.

4 a How do people usually celebrate the festival? Give **two** details in **English**.

1. ....

2. .... *[2 marks]*

4 b How does Mehdi's family celebrate Eid?

A	The children wear their new clothes.
B	The adults give the children presents.
C	The whole family goes out together.
D	They listen to traditional music and dance.

Choose the two correct statements. Write the correct letters in the boxes.

☐ ☐

[2 marks]

Theme 2 — Mixed Practice

5 You will hear 4 short sentences. Listen carefully and, using your knowledge of French sounds, write down in **French** exactly what you hear for each sentence.

You will hear each sentence **three** times: the first time as a full sentence, the second time in short sections and the third time again as a full sentence.

Use your knowledge of French sounds and grammar to make sure that what you have written makes sense. Check carefully that your spelling is accurate.

5 a Sentence 1

....

.... *[2 marks]*

5 b Sentence 2

....

.... *[2 marks]*

5 c Sentence 3

....

.... *[2 marks]*

5 d Sentence 4

....

.... *[2 marks]*

6 When your teacher asks you, read aloud the following text **in French**.

> C'est la fête de Noël ce vendredi.
>
> Je pense que c'est mon événement préféré car tous mes amis sont là.
>
> L'année dernière, j'ai aidé à préparer un gâteau traditionnel.
>
> Cette année, nous allons danser et chanter beaucoup de chansons.
>
> Je voudrais regarder le feu d'artifice avant minuit.

- You will then be asked four questions **in French** that relate to the topic of **Popular culture**.
- In order to score the highest marks, **answer all four questions as fully as you can**.

[15 marks]

7 You read this article about a sports event. Answer the questions below **in English**.

> *Chaque année, il y a un événement sportif à la Réunion qui s'appelle Le Grand Raid. En octobre, près de 2500 personnes arrivent sur l'île pour participer à ce concours. Il y a une course qui commence dans le sud de l'île au bord de la mer. Normalement, les gens courent pendant plus de vingt-quatre heures pour finir cette course — c'est environ cent soixante-cinq kilomètres. Il y a aussi quatre autres courses, donc il faut suivre **les balises** de la couleur du chemin que vous allez prendre.*

7 a How often does the event happen?

.... *[1 mark]*

7 b Where does the race start? Give **two** details.

1. ....

2. .... *[2 marks]*

7 c How much time does it usually take to complete the race?

.... *[1 mark]*

7 d Read the last sentence again. What are **les balises**? Write the correct letter in the box.

A	water points
B	paths
C	markers

[1 mark]

8 A celebrity couple were interviewed on the red carpet at an event. Listen to the interview and complete the sentences in **English**.

8 a Sabrina thinks the prize might go to Sylvie because...

.... *[1 mark]*

8 b Patrick and Sabrina's new house is located...

.... *[1 mark]*

8 c Sabrina and her group have plans to...

1. ....

2. .... *[2 marks]*

Score:

Theme 2 — Mixed Practice

Mixed Practice — Higher

1 Read Ahmed's email to his friend. Answer the questions below in **English**.

> Bonjour Diane,
>
> Comme tu le sais, la musique est ma passion. J'écoute divers genres de musique et c'est mon rêve d'apprendre à jouer d'un instrument. Cet été, je vais à un festival de musique en Angleterre avec mon cousin. On a acheté nos billets pour le festival, mais on doit encore organiser le transport et le logement. Si j'ai le temps, j'irai à Londres pour passer quelques jours chez toi. Je voudrais aller voir un match de foot au stade de Wembley et manger dans le restaurant d'un chef célèbre. Je ne dois pas oublier de t'envoyer les dates de notre voyage !
>
> À bientôt !

1 a What is Ahmed's dream?

.... *[1 mark]*

1 b What **two** things do Ahmed and his cousin still need to organise?

1. ....

2. .... *[2 marks]*

1 c Give **two** things Ahmed wants to do in London.

1. ....

2. .... *[2 marks]*

2 You are writing an article for a local newspaper. Your article is about festivals and events. Write about **150** words in **French**. You must write something about both bullet points.

Describe:

- the importance of festivals and traditions
- a festival or event that you went to recently. *[25 marks]*

3 You are talking to your Swiss friend. Your teacher will play the part of your friend and will speak first.

- You should address your friend as *tu*.
- When you see this – ? – you will have to ask a question.

In order to score full marks, you must include a verb in your response to each task.

1. Describe your favourite hobby. (Give **one** detail and **one** reason.)
2. Say when you do this hobby. (Give **one** detail.)
3. Say what your least favourite activity is and why. (Give **one** opinion and **one** reason.)
? 4. Ask your friend a question about what they do in their free time.
5. Say what you usually do with your friends. (Give **two** details.)

[10 marks]

4 Translate the following sentences **into French**.

4 a You want to go to the French restaurant.

....

.... *[2 marks]*

4 b I won a national competition with my new song.

....

.... *[2 marks]*

4 c His photos encourage people to be more positive.

....

.... *[2 marks]*

4 d She often posts videos about her job on social networks.

....

.... *[2 marks]*

4 e This week, I will organise an event to celebrate the success of a local artist.

....

.... *[2 marks]*

5

You read an article Richard has written about his career.

> L'année prochaine, je créerai ma propre émission de cuisine pour la télé. Ma carrière a commencé à l'âge de seize ans quand j'ai préparé mes premiers plats et trouvé un emploi à Paris. Aujourd'hui, je suis chef à Londres* et propriètaire de plusieurs restaurants. Je travaille sept jours sur sept et je gagne peu d'argent, mais j'ai gardé la passion de la cuisine. Je viens d'ouvrir mon deuxième restaurant et actuellement je suis en train d'écrire un livre de recettes.
> *Londres = London

What does the article say about these events?

Write **P** for something that happened **in the past**

N for something that is happening **now**

F for something that will happen **in the future**.

Write the correct letter in each box.

5 a Creating a TV show ☐ *[1 mark]*

5 b Moving to Paris ☐ *[1 mark]*

5 c Working seven days a week ☐ *[1 mark]*

5 d Opening a second restaurant ☐ *[1 mark]*

5 e Writing a recipe book ☐ *[1 mark]*

6

While in a café in Brussels, you overhear two people talking about what they are watching on TV. Complete the sentences **in English**.

6 a Camille watched a show about ...

.... *[1 mark]*

6 b She thought it had...

.... *[1 mark]*

6 c Alex will watch a show about...

.... *[1 mark]*

6 d He appreciates...

.... *[1 mark]*

Score: ☐

Section Nine — Travel and Tourism

Where to Go, Accommodation and Travel

1   Spend a few minutes looking at the two photos. Make notes on them to use during the test.

Your teacher will ask you to talk about the content of the photos. You should talk for approximately **one and a half minutes**. **You must say at least one thing about each photo.**

Scan the QR code to hear the teacher part of the question, or you can find the transcript in the back of the book.

After you have spoken about the content of the photos, your teacher will then ask you questions related to **any** of the topics within the theme of **Communication and the world around us**.

[25 marks]

2   Listen to these French students talking about their holidays. Choose the **two** correct statements for each student and write the correct letters in the boxes.

2 a Yasmina:

A	She spends her holidays with her family.
B	She knows the area so doesn't need a map.
C	She buys food before she goes on holiday.
D	She goes to the mountains.

[2 marks]

2 b Mehdi:

A	He enjoys camping.
B	He doesn't have to pay for his holidays.
C	He likes holidays in the countryside.
D	He enjoys trying regional food.

[2 marks]

2 c Chloé:

A	The apartment didn't cost a lot.
B	The toilets were broken.
C	The bedrooms were clean.
D	She will go back next year.

[2 marks]

3 Read this online advert for holiday jobs.

> Vous avez beaucoup de temps libre pendant les vacances d'été ?
>
> Les jeunes en France partent souvent en vacances avec leur famille parce qu'ils pensent que partir seul coûte cher.
>
> Alors, vous êtes un de ces jeunes qui n'ont pas beaucoup d'argent ? Pourquoi ne pas trouver un boulot d'été ? Vous pouvez travailler comme serveur à l'étranger. Comme ça, vous pouvez apprendre une autre langue et gagner un peu d'argent en même temps.

Answer the following questions in **English**.

3 a According to the advert, why do young French people often choose to go on holiday with their parents?

.... *[1 mark]*

3 b What job does the advert suggest that young people do?

.... *[1 mark]*

3 c What does the advert say are the **two** advantages of holiday jobs?

1. ....

2. .... *[2 marks]*

4 You are writing a post for a holiday website. Your post is about making travel plans.
Write about **150** words in **French**.
You must write something about both bullet points.

Describe:

- the importance of researching a holiday before going
- the accommodation you would like to stay at in the future and why. *[25 marks]*

Score:

What to Do

1 Read these online reviews of a local museum and answer the questions below.

> **Léa**: Je ne recommande pas ce musée — il est assez cher et je l'ai trouvé ennuyeux.
> **Dorian**: Si vous êtes au centre-ville, vous devez visiter le musée. Il est plein d'objets intéressants qui viennent du passé. C'est une visite vraiment agréable.
> **Fathia**: Le musée est une bonne idée s'il pleut, mais s'il fait beau, je préfère passer mon temps à la campagne.

Match the correct person with each of the following questions.
Write **L** for **Léa**, **D** for **Dorian** or **F** for **Fathia**. Write the correct letter in each box.

1 a Who thinks the museum is **sometimes** worth visiting? ☐ *[1 mark]*

1 b Who thinks the museum is **definitely** worth visiting? ☐ *[1 mark]*

1 c Who feels that the museum is **not** worth visiting? ☐ *[1 mark]*

2 You will hear 4 short sentences. Listen carefully and, using your knowledge of French sounds, write down in **French** exactly what you hear for each sentence.

You will hear each sentence **three** times: the first time as a full sentence, the second time in short sections and the third time again as a full sentence.

Use your knowledge of French sounds and grammar to make sure that what you have written makes sense. Check carefully that your spelling is accurate.

2 a Sentence 1

.... *[2 marks]*

2 b Sentence 2

....

.... *[2 marks]*

2 c Sentence 3

....

.... *[2 marks]*

2 d Sentence 4

....

.... *[2 marks]*

3 You are writing an email to your friend about your holiday activities.
Write approximately **90** words in **French**.
You must write something about each bullet point.

Describe:
- what you did during your last holiday
- your opinion on going to the beach
- a city you will visit in the future.

[15 marks]

4 Translate the following sentences into **French**.

4 a I make the most of my holidays abroad each year.

....

.... *[2 marks]*

4 b This afternoon, I will swim in the quiet lake near our hotel.

....

.... *[2 marks]*

4 c My mother ordered a drink and an ice cream.

....

.... *[2 marks]*

4 d He decided to accompany me to the market.

....

.... *[2 marks]*

4 e The former central station is now a modern art museum.

....

.... *[2 marks]*

Score:

Section Ten — Media and Technology

Technology and The Internet

1 Listen to this radio debate about technology. Complete the sentences in **English**.

1 a Fatima likes technnology because...

.... *[1 mark]*

She uses an app to...

.... *[1 mark]*

1 b Mohamed thinks that young people...

.... *[1 mark]*

He thinks it's impossible to avoid...

.... *[1 mark]*

2 Read what these French students have to say about technology.

> **Axel**: Je crois qu'il y a trop de commentaires négatifs sur les blogs en ligne — c'est un problème car, à mon avis, ça rend les réseaux sociaux moins agréables.
> **Eva**: Moi, j'adore faire des achats en ligne parce que c'est moins cher que les magasins dans ma ville. Cependant, le résultat sera que les entreprises locales fermeront.
> **Charlie**: J'ai beaucoup d'applications pour tous mes différents passe-temps — c'est très utile de les avoir sur mon portable, et généralement, elles sont gratuites à télécharger.
> **Hugo**: Je profite des sites de streaming chaque soir. Il y a quelque chose pour toute la famille. Malheureusement, ça coûte beaucoup d'argent.

What do these students think about different aspects of technology?

Write **P** for a **positive** opinion

N for a **negative** opinion

P + N for a **positive** and **negative** opinion.

Write the correct letter in each box.

2 a Axel ☐ *[1 mark]*

2 b Eva ☐ *[1 mark]*

2 c Charlie ☐ *[1 mark]*

2 d Hugo ☐ *[1 mark]*

3 Translate the following sentences into **French**.

3 a I have a laptop.

....

.... *[2 marks]*

3 b I prefer to buy clothes online.

....

.... *[2 marks]*

3 c There are lots of games and films on my computer.

....

.... *[2 marks]*

3 d I am going to send the email tomorrow.

....

.... *[2 marks]*

3 e Yesterday, my telephone did not work.

....

.... *[2 marks]*

4 You are writing a review of the apps you use every day.
Write about **150** words in **French**.
You must write something about both bullet points.

Describe:

- the different types of apps you use and why
- a new app you downloaded recently. *[25 marks]*

Score:

Section Ten — Media and Technology

Social Media

1 Read this text about Camille's digital detox.

> Je passe au moins quatre heures chaque jour sur les réseaux sociaux. J'ai commencé à les utiliser pour chatter avec mes amis. Maintenant, je regarde beaucoup de courtes vidéos. Ce mois, je n'utilise pas les réseaux sociaux. Cette semaine je passe plus de temps avec ma famille et je lis plus chaque soir, c'est géniale car je dors mieux et j'ai moins de soucis.

Answer the questions below in **English**.

1 a How much time does Camille spend on social media every day?

.... *[1 mark]*

1 b What does Camille now use social media for?

.... *[1 mark]*

1 c Name **one** thing Camille does this week, and **one** effect it has on her life.

....

.... *[2 marks]*

2 Read what these three young people have to say about social media.

> **Jade**: Les réseaux sociaux sont un bon endroit pour avoir des conversations importantes. Ils peuvent créer une grande famille de gens qui partagent les mêmes intérêts.
> **Alex**: Les photos des célébrités ont trop d'influence sur notre génération et je crois que les ados postent des selfies sans penser à leur sécurité.
> **Toni**: Les fausses informations sont toujours disponibles en ligne, donc j'essaie de ne pas passer trop de temps sur les réseaux sociaux.

What topic does each person mention?

Write **J** for **Jade**
     A for **Alex**
     T for **Toni**.

Write the correct letter in the box.

2 a Fake news   ☐ *[1 marks]*

2 b Community   ☐ *[1 marks]*

2 c Online safety   ☐ *[1 marks]*

2 d Avoiding social media   ☐ *[1 marks]*

Section Ten — Media and Technology

3 A group of people are recording a podcast. What is in this photo? Write **five** sentences in **French**.

3 a .... *[2 marks]*

3 b .... *[2 marks]*

3 c .... *[2 marks]*

3 d .... *[2 marks]*

3 e .... *[2 marks]*

4 Listen to these interviews about social media. For each person, choose the correct statement. Write the correct letter in each box.

4 a Clara:

A	She prefers to talk to her best friend in person.
B	She shares photos with her friends online.
C	She talks to her best friend every day.

[1 mark]

4 b Jules:

A	He prefers to keep his pictures and videos private.
B	He likes to show people what he's been doing.
C	He doesn't follow many influencers.

[1 mark]

4 c Chloé:

A	She never uses social media.
B	Her school gave students tips on staying safe online.
C	She believes the internet isn't dangerous.

[1 mark]

5 You are writing an article for the school newsletter on the dangers of social media. Write about **90** words in **French**. You must write something about each bullet point.

Describe:

- how you use social media
- a recent negative experience online
- how young people can avoid the dangers of social media in the future.

[15 marks]

Score:

Where You Live and The Home

1 You hear some French students talking about their local area. What is the opinion of the students on the following aspects?

Write **P** for a **positive** opinion

N for a **negative** opinion

P + N for a **positive** and **negative** opinion.

1 a Public spaces [1 mark]

1 b Transport [1 mark]

1 c Town centre [1 mark]

1 d Things to do [1 mark]

2 You read this message from your friend Sylvie about her plans to move.

> Je viens du Canada, mais maintenant j'habite dans la capitale de la France. J'ai un nouvel emploi donc je vais acheter un appartement près du bureau. Je veux habiter dans un quartier sûr et calme parce que j'habite seule. Mon nouveau logement doit avoir un jardin car j'adore les fleurs.
>
> **Sylvie**

Answer the following questions in **English**.

2 a Where did Sylvie used to live?

.... [1 mark]

2 b Why is Sylvie moving?

.... [1 mark]

2 c Why does Sylvie want to live in a safe area of town?

.... [1 mark]

2 d What feature must Sylvie's new accommodation have?

.... [1 mark]

3 You are writing a blog post about home life.
Write approximately **90** words in **French**.
You must write something about each bullet point.

Describe:
- the rooms in your current home
- an activity you did at home recently
- where you would like to live in the future.

[15 marks]

4 Translate the following sentences into **French**.

4 a I live in a small town in England.

....

.... *[2 marks]*

4 b The house is situated in the south of France.

....

.... *[2 marks]*

4 c There are three bedrooms, a beautiful kitchen and a garden.

....

.... *[2 marks]*

4 d I used to live in the suburbs of the capital city.

....

.... *[2 marks]*

4 e It's my dream to build a house next to a lake.

....

.... *[2 marks]*

Score:

The Local Area, Directions and Weather

1 You are talking to your friend from Quebec.
Your teacher will play the part of your friend and will speak first.

- You should address your friend as *tu*.
- When you see this – **?** – you will have to ask a question.

> **In order to score full marks, you must include a verb in your response to each task.**
>
> 1. Describe your town or village. (Give **one** detail.)
> 2. Say where you like to go in town. (Give **one** detail.)
> 3. Give **one** opinion of your local area.
> **?** 4. Ask your friend a question about where they live. (Give **one** detail.)
> 5. Describe the weather in your area. (Give **one** detail.)

[10 marks]

2 You hear an interview at your local shopping centre with three shoppers, Ahmed, Dorian and Nadia.
Listen to their responses, then answer the questions in **English**.

2 a Why did Ahmed come to the shopping centre?

.... *[1 mark]*

2 b Why does Ahmed prefer to do his food shopping there?

....

.... *[1 mark]*

2 c Why didn't Nadia buy anything?

.... *[1 mark]*

2 d What is Nadia looking for now?

.... *[1 mark]*

2 e What does Dorian think of shopping at the centre? Give **two** details.

1. ....

2. .... *[2 marks]*

Section Eleven — Where People Live

3 Translate the following sentences into **English**.

3 a Le stade se trouve devant la gare.

....

.... *[2 marks]*

3 b Mes amis me disent que j'habite trop loin de la ville.

....

.... *[2 marks]*

3 c Le climat est relativement chaud et il pleut moins souvent.

....

.... *[2 marks]*

3 d Selon la météo, il y aura de la neige la semaine prochaine.

....

.... *[2 marks]*

3 e Quand j'étais jeune, j'habitais dans l'ouest de la région.

....

.... *[2 marks]*

4 You are writing an email to your French friend about your region and the climate there. Write approximately **90** words in **French**. You must write something about each bullet point.

Describe:

- where your region is located in your country
- what the weather has been like over the past year
- a way in which your region will change in the future. *[15 marks]*

Score:

Section Twelve — Environmental and Social Issues

Protecting the Environment & Environmental Problems

 1 Listen to this extract from a podcast on recycling. Answer the questions in **English**.

1 a According to the podcast, why is recycling important?

.... *[1 mark]*

1 b What should people do to help? Give **two** details.

1. ....

2. .... *[2 marks]*

1 c Name **two** things mentioned in the podcast that can be recycled.

1. ....

2. .... *[2 marks]*

2 Read this website post that Sofiane wrote about traffic in Nice.

> À Nice, il y a beaucoup de pollution à cause de la circulation. Il y a toujours trop de voitures et c'est mauvais pour la santé. Selon moi, le gouvernement a une responsabilité — il doit réduire le niveau de pollution en créant des espaces verts au centre-ville. Mais c'est à nous aussi de prendre des mesures. Par exemple, on peut aller au travail à pied ou prendre le train ou l'autobus. S'il est vraiment nécessaire de conduire pour aller au travail, on peut partager une voiture avec des collègues.

Which of the following does Sofiane suggest as solutions to the high levels of pollution in Nice? Write the letters in the boxes.

A	banning cars in the city centre
B	increasing the number of green spaces
C	improving the speed of public transport
D	encouraging people to car share

[2 marks]

3 Using your knowledge of grammar, complete the following sentences in **French**.
Choose the correct French word from the three options in the grid.
Write the correct **word** in the space.

3 a On .... utiliser les transports publics.

| peut | peux | pouvons |

[1 mark]

3 b Beaucoup d'........................ sont en danger.

| animal | animaux | animals |

[1 mark]

4 Spend a few minutes looking at the two photos.
Make notes on them to use during the test.

Your teacher will ask you to talk about the content of the photos.
You should talk for approximately **one and a half minutes**.
You must say at least one thing about each photo.

After you have spoken about the content of the photos, your teacher will
then ask you questions related to **any** of the topics within the theme of
Communication and the world around us.

[25 marks]

5 You are writing a post for a French environmental blog.
Your post is about climate change. Write about **150** words in **French**.
You must write something about both bullet points.

Describe:

- what we can do to reduce pollution levels

- what you will do in future to look after the planet.

[25 marks]

Score:

Social Issues

1 You are writing a letter to the manager of a French charity shop to apply for a job as a volunteer.
Write approximately **90** words in **French**.
You must write something about each bullet point.

Describe:

- why you want to help
- the volunteer work you have already done
- how you will help the association.

[15 marks]

2 Translate the following sentences into **French**.

2 a There is a demonstration in my town today.

....

.... *[2 marks]*

2 b The citizens are fighting for equality between men and women.

....

.... *[2 marks]*

2 c Next week, I will organise a debate about politics at school.

....

.... *[2 marks]*

2 d The level of violence in the streets was a shock for me.

....

.... *[2 marks]*

2 e Last night, the new president's spokesperson announced his victory.

....

.... *[2 marks]*

Section Twelve — Environmental and Social Issues

3 Read what these people have to say about the problems they face in their local area.

> **Yanis:** Le tourisme est essentiel dans ma région mais pendant certaines saisons il n'y a pas beaucoup de travail. À mon avis, le chômage est un problème grave.
> **Inès:** J'habite dans la capitale, et tous les jours je vois des gens qui dorment dans la rue. C'est inquiétant car la société peut faire plus pour améliorer la situation.
> **Hugo:** Ma ville n'est pas très sûre — récemment il y avait plus de violence dans les rues. Je voudrais donc devenir bénévole pour aider mes voisins.

Match the correct person with each of the following questions.
Write **Y** for **Yanis**, **I** for **Inès** or **H** for **Hugo**. Write the correct letter in each box.

3 a Who lives in an unsafe area? [1 mark]

3 b Who thinks that unemployment is the main problem? [1 mark]

3 c Who mentions homelessness? [1 mark]

3 d Who would like to do more to help? [1 mark]

3 e Who lives in a holiday destination? [1 mark]

4 Listen to this French news report.
Write the correct letters in the boxes to complete the sentences.

4 a In Lyon, it took three hours to...

A	stop the violence.
B	break up the protest.
C	find all the injured victims.

[1 mark]

4 b The goal of the charity event in Paris was...

A	to encourage people to do sport.
B	to raise money for associations.
C	to support families living in poverty.

[1 mark]

4 c The crisis in the south of France was caused by...

A	a week's worth of rainfall in 12 hours.
B	a lack of rainfall for a month.
C	a month's worth of rainfall in 24 hours.

[1 mark]

Score:

Section Twelve — Environmental and Social Issues

Mixed Practice — Foundation

1. You read this diary entry about a holiday in Morocco.

> *Ce soir, on va manger dans un restaurant du quartier. Après le repas, je vais me coucher tôt parce qu'on est arrivé au Maroc tard hier soir. En ce moment, on est à la plage et puis on va visiter un musée.*

What does the diary say about these events?

Write **P** for something that happened **in the past**
     N for something that is happening **now**
       F for something that will happen **in the future**.

Write the correct letter in each box.

1 a Eating out   *[1 mark]*

1 b Going to bed early   *[1 mark]*

1 c Arriving in Morocco   *[1 mark]*

1 d Spending time at the beach   *[1 mark]*

1 e Visiting a museum   *[1 mark]*

2. Spend a few minutes looking at the two photos.
Make notes on them to use during the test.

Your teacher will ask you to talk about the content of the photos. You should talk for approximately **one minute**. **You must say at least one thing about each photo.**

After you have spoken about the content of the photos, your teacher will then ask you questions related to any of the topics within the theme of **The world around us.**

[25 marks]

3 Translate the following sentences **into French**.

3 a What is your address please?

....

.... *[2 marks]*

3 b I like the countryside because it is quiet.

....

.... *[2 marks]*

3 c We went to my sister's shop yesterday.

....

.... *[2 marks]*

3 d There is a lack of libraries in my town.

....

.... *[2 marks]*

3 e I live in the north of England.

....

.... *[2 marks]*

4 When your teacher asks you, read aloud the following text **in French**.

> J'utilise mon portable tous les jours.
>
> Il y a beaucoup d'applications utiles.
>
> Je chatte avec mes amis sur les médias sociaux.
>
> Ma copine adore acheter des vêtements en ligne.
>
> Elle aime le streaming car elle peut regarder des films.

- You will then be asked four questions **in French** that relate to the topic of **Media and technology**.

- In order to score the highest marks, **answer all four questions as fully as you can**.

[15 marks]

5 You overhear two French students talking about where they live. Why do they **not** like where they live?

A	neighbours
B	roads
C	things to do
D	location
E	house
F	weather

Write the correct letter in each box.

5 a   Reason 1 ☐   Reason 2 ☐

[1 mark]

5 b   Reason 3 ☐   Reason 4 ☐

[1 mark]

6 You are on holiday and writing a postcard to your friends.
Write a short description of your holiday for them.
Write approximately **50** words in **French**.
You must write something about each bullet point.

Mention:
- your accommodation
- who you have gone with
- the weather
- how you got there
- what you are doing there.

[10 marks]

7 You are talking to your French friend. Your teacher will play the part of your friend and will speak first.

- You should address your friend as *tu*.
- When you see this – **?** – you will have to ask a question.

In order to score full marks, you must include a verb in your response to each task.

1. Describe where your house or flat is located. (Give **one** detail.)
2. Give your opinion of your local area. (Give **one** detail.)
? 3. Ask your friend where they live.
4. Say why you like your house or flat. (Give **one** detail.)
5. Describe what there is to do in your area. (Give **one** detail.)

[10 marks]

8 You see some headlines on a French news website.

A	La violence dans les rues augmente
B	La faim est partout
C	Les ressources naturelles diminuent
D	Le plastique : pas pour la poubelle
E	Sans emploi, sans maison

Which headline matches each idea?

Write the correct letter in each box.

8 a Unemployment

[1 mark]

8 b Social unrest

[1 mark]

8 c Hunger

[1 mark]

9 A family is using technology.
What is in this photo?
Write **five** sentences in **French**.

9 a .... *[2 marks]*

9 b .... *[2 marks]*

9 c .... *[2 marks]*

9 d .... *[2 marks]*

9 e .... *[2 marks]*

Score:

Mixed Practice — Both Tiers

1 Read these reviews of a hotel and answer the questions below.

> *Patrick:* La chambre était sale, mais la vue était géniale.
>
> *Eva:* Je suis arrivée au logement et j'avais réservé une chambre, mais l'hôtel était complet. C'était une mauvaise expérience.
>
> *Clara:* L'hôtel n'était pas trop cher et j'ai bien dormi. Il se situe dans un super endroit près de beaucoup de bons restaurants.

Match the correct person with each of the following questions.
Write **P** for **Patrick**, **E** for **Eva** or **C** for **Clara**. Write the correct letter in each box.

1 a Who mentions the hotel's location? *[1 mark]*

1 b Who has a mixed opinion of the hotel? *[1 mark]*

1 c Who says the hotel was fully booked? *[1 mark]*

1 d Who mentions the cost of the hotel? *[1 mark]*

1 e Whose room was dirty? *[1 mark]*

2 You read a blog about living abroad.
Answer the questions **in English**.

> Vivre à l'étranger peut être difficile car parfois la communication n'est pas simple. Cependant, on a aussi de bonnes surprises parce qu'on peut découvrir de nouveaux intérêts. C'est également une occasion d'apprendre une nouvelle langue et de rencontrer beaucoup de gens différents de tous les coins du monde.

2 a Why is living abroad hard?

.... *[1 mark]*

2 b What might be a surprise when living abroad?

.... *[1 mark]*

2 c What are **two** other benefits of living abroad?

1. ....

2. .... *[2 marks]*

3 You will hear 4 short sentences. Listen carefully and, using your knowledge of French sounds, write down in **French** exactly what you hear for each sentence.

You will hear each sentence **three** times: the first time as a full sentence, the second time in short sections and the third time again as a full sentence.

Use your knowledge of French sounds and grammar to make sure that what you have written makes sense. Check carefully that your spelling is accurate.

3 a   Sentence 1

   ....

   .... *[2 marks]*

3 b   Sentence 2

   ....

   .... *[2 marks]*

3 c   Sentence 3

   ....

   .... *[2 marks]*

3 d   Sentence 4 (Higher)

   ....

   .... *[2 marks]*

4 You are writing a letter to your friend about social issues.
Write approximately **90** words in **French**.
You must write something about each bullet point.

Describe:

- a time that you helped someone
- your opinion on unemployment
- how we can reduce poverty in the future. *[15 marks]*

Score:

Mixed Practice — Higher

1 Listen to this phone call about a French tourist attraction. Then answer the questions in **English.**

1 a Which tourist attraction does the caller talk about?

.... *[1 mark]*

1 b What mode of transport can't you use to get to the attraction?

.... *[1 mark]*

1 c Give two other details about visiting the site.

1. ....

2. .... *[2 marks]*

2 You read this email about Tom's house move.

> *Dans quelques mois, je retournerai vivre dans la cité où j'ai grandi parce que ma mère est malade. J'ai quitté la ville l'année dernière pour vivre à la campagne car j'adore la nature. Je suis un peu inquiet, parce que je n'étais jamais tranquille en ville. Cependant, mes amis me manquent beaucoup et je vais être heureux de les voir bientôt.*

What does Tom say about these events?

Write **P** for something that happened **in the past**
    N for something that is happening **now**
    F for something that will happen **in the future**.

Write the correct letter in each box.

2 a Returning to the council estate   ☐ *[1 mark]*

2 b His mum's illness   ☐ *[1 mark]*

2 c Leaving his hometown   ☐ *[1 mark]*

2 d Feeling concerned   ☐ *[1 mark]*

2 e Seeing friends   ☐ *[1 mark]*

3 You hear some news stories on the radio.

3 a

A	There are many delayed trains.
B	People should buy their tickets early.
C	People should avoid travelling at all.
D	Trains may not stop at every station.

Choose the **two** correct statements
Write the correct letters in the boxes.

☐ ☐

[2 marks]

3 b

A	Most people think young people shouldn't be online.
B	More adults are joining online communities.
C	Social media is popular amongst young people.
D	Online bullying is a big problem.

Choose the **two** correct statements
Write the correct letters in the boxes.

☐ ☐

[2 marks]

3 c

A	Species are slowly disappearing.
B	Forest fires are causing animal deaths.
C	Different habitats are flooding.
D	The situation is getting worse.

Choose the **two** correct statements
Write the correct letters in the boxes.

☐ ☐

[2 marks]

4 You are writing an article about online shopping.
Write approximately **150** words in **French**.
You must write something about both bullet points.

Describe:

• the positive and negative aspects of online shopping

• something you bought online recently.

[25 marks]

5 While listening to the radio, you hear a weather forecast. Complete the sentences **in English**.

5 a On Monday, it will be chilly in...

.... *[1 mark]*

5 b Tuesday will see snow in every part of...

.... *[1 mark]*

5 c On Wednesday, it will be raining in...

.... *[1 mark]*

5 d On Thursday, people in Corsica can expect the weather to be...

.... *[1 mark]*

6 Translate the following sentences into **English**.

6 a Recharge ton portable — je t'ai envoyé un message.

....

.... *[2 marks]*

6 b La protection contre les attaques en ligne est très importante.

....

.... *[2 marks]*

6 c Le consommateur peut facilement renvoyer son achat s'il y a un problème.

....

.... *[2 marks]*

6 d Sur les réseaux sociaux, tu peux aimer une image et ajouter un commentaire.

....

.... *[2 marks]*

6 e J'ai cassé mon ordinateur, alors j'achèterai un nouvel appareil bientôt.

....

.... *[2 marks]*

7 Listen to this French podcast about a girl found in the wild. Choose the correct answer and write the letter in each box.

7 a The girl was found...

A	after one year.
B	in a field.
C	near a town.

[1 mark]

7 b She had been sleeping...

A	on the cold floor.
B	in an ancient forest.
C	in an old tower.

[1 mark]

7 c She stayed healthy by...

A	eating vegetables.
B	finding a hospital.
C	washing her food.

[1 mark]

7 d When she grew up, she started...

A	looking after birds.
B	working in healthcare.
C	studying plants.

[1 mark]

8 When your teacher asks you, read aloud the following text **in French**.

> Il y a toujours beaucoup de crimes en temps de guerre.
>
> Les soldats utilisent des armes pour attaquer l'ennemi.
>
> Ces conflits causent de la souffrance pour l'humanité.
>
> Il y a des bénévoles qui aident les victimes et sauvent des vies.
>
> Il faut défendre la paix en manifestant ensemble.

- You will then be asked four questions **in French** that relate to the topic of **The world around us**.

- In order to score the highest marks, **answer all four questions as fully as you can**.

[15 marks]

Score:

Nouns and Articles

1 Underline all of the nouns in the sentences below.

- **a** Elle aime manger des fruits.
- **b** Le professeur a une nouvelle voiture.
- **c** On parle français au Canada.
- **d** J'ai reçu une lettre de Sofiane.
- **e** Les gens dansent.
- **f** C'est le sac de ma mère.
- **g** Manon a acheté des frites.
- **h** La poste est ouverte.
- **i** Le film n'est pas amusant.
- **j** Marie habite près de mon frère.

2 Write either **m** or **f** after each noun to show whether it is masculine or feminine.

- **a** choix ....
- **b** boulot ....
- **c** thé ....
- **d** salle ....
- **e** stage ....
- **f** lit ....
- **g** capitale ....
- **h** copain ....
- **i** village ....
- **j** pays ....
- **k** maison ....
- **l** ville ....
- **m** stylo ....
- **n** ciel ....
- **o** frère ....
- **p** défilé ....

3 Write down the plural form of each noun, then translate them into English. Not all of them need to change.

- **a** tableau ....
- **b** parc ....
- **c** fils ....
- **d** feu ....
- **e** prix ....
- **f** lieu ....
- **g** journal ....
- **h** homme ....
- **i** château ....
- **j** bureau ....

4 Fill in the gaps in these sentences with the plural form of the word in the brackets.

- **a** Il y a trois .... entre le stade et l'hôpital. **(rue)**
- **b** Mes amis aiment faire du sport, mais je préfère jouer à des .... **(jeu)**
- **c** Je vais souvent au zoo car j'aime bien voir les .... **(animal)**
- **d** Il faut manger des fruits et des .... tous les jours. **(légume)**
- **e** Je dois acheter des .... pour ma famille. **(cadeau)**

5 Circle the correct definite articles (**le, la, l'** or **les**) to complete the sentences below.

    a   **Les** / **Le** filles aiment jouer au foot.

    b   Ce soir, **le** / **les** repas va être traditionnel.

    c   Fermez **la** / **les** porte, s'il vous plaît.

    d   Nous avons trouvé tous **les** / **le** sacs sous **la** / **le** table.

    e   **Le** / **L'** hôtel est à côté de chez moi.

6 Fill in the gaps in these sentences using the correct indefinite article (**un** or **une**).

    a   J'ai acheté .... café, ... gâteau et .... boisson.

    b   Ma mère a .... sœur et .... cousin.

    c   Dans mon jardin, il y a .... arbre, ... pont et trois chaises.

7 Translate these sentences into **French**.

    a   I'm going to the beach.   ....

    b   He will visit Morocco.   ....

    c   She has an aunt and an uncle.   ....

8 Fill in the gaps in these sentences using the correct partitive article from the box.

    a   Sylvie a .... cousins.   **e**   Elle mange beaucoup .... fromage.

    b   Je n'ai pas .... livre.   **f**   Richard n'a pas .... portable.

    c   Ils ont gagné .... argent.   **g**   Il me donne .... glace.

    d   Il prend .... poisson.   **h**   Je veux .... billets.

> de
> du
> de la
> de l'
> des

9 Translate these sentences into **French**.

    a   I'm going to Senegal this year.

          ....

    b   He comes from England.

          ....

Pronouns

1 Fill in the gaps in the second sentences with the right pronoun.

Example: Sabrina est professeur. *Elle* va chaque jour au collège.

a Mon chien est malade. .... ne mange pas beaucoup.

b Leur tante est médecin. .... travaille dans un hôpital.

c Mes sœurs aiment les festivals de musique. .... ont acheté des billets.

d Ses parents sont en vacances. .... vont rentrer à la maison la semaine prochaine.

2 Fill in the gaps with the correct indirect object pronoun from the box. Use the English translation to help you.

You might have to shorten me to m' and te to t'.

	je	tu	il / elle	nous	vous	ils / elles
indirect object pronouns	me	te	lui	nous	vous	leur

a Tu .... as donné de l'eau. — *You have given her some water.*

b Il .... a apporté ton cahier. — *He brought me your exercise book.*

c Je .... ai déjà parlé. — *I have spoken to you already. (informal singular)*

d Nous .... avons tout expliqué. — *We explained everything to you. (plural)*

H e Elle .... a acheté un cadeau. — *She has bought us a present.*

3 Fill in the gaps in these sentences with the correct emphatic pronoun. Use the clues in brackets to help you.

a Il est sorti avec .... (**me**)

b Elles ont écrit la chanson pour .... (**you**, *informal singular*)

H c Ils le font .... -mêmes. (**themselves**)

d Il y est allé .... -même. (**himself**)

4 Translate these questions into **French** using the interrogative pronouns **qui**, **que** and **quoi**.

a Who is singing? ....

b What are you thinking about? ....

c What do you do at the weekend? ....

d Who can help me with this exercise? ....

Section Thirteen — Nouns, Articles and Linking Words

5 Fill in the gaps in these sentences with **qui**, **que** or **qu'**.

Example: Le chien .... *qui* .... a mangé mon déjeuner est malade.

a Le garçon .... porte un uniforme est très travailleur.

b Le repas .... tu as préparé était bon.

c C'est un homme .... aime le fromage.

d Le touriste .... ils ont vu était célèbre.

e Les vêtements .... elle achète sont extraordinaires.

f La personne .... m'a volé la voiture était vieille.

6 Translate these indefinite pronouns into **French**.

a something   ....

b everything   ....

c someone   ....

d everyone   ....

e several   ....

f each one   ....

7 Translate each of these sentences into **English**.

a Ça ne m'intéresse pas beaucoup.

   ....

b Cela me fait rire.

   ....

c Ceci peut nous aider à faire les exercices.

   ....

8 Each of these sentences is missing a pronoun.
Choose **y** or **en** to fill in the gaps.

a J'adore la plage. On .... va quand il fait beau.

b J'ai besoin de lait. Est-ce que tu peux m' .... acheter ?

c Je voudrais visiter le musée mais tu .... es déjà allée.

d As-tu du pain? Je n' .... ai plus.

Find the CGP RevisionHub at cgpbooks.co.uk/cafe   Section Thirteen — Nouns, Articles and Linking Words

Conjunctions and Prepositions

1 Translate these conjunctions into **English**.

a puis .... f ensuite .... k par exemple ....

b si .... g comme .... l parce que ....

c mais .... h cependant .... m puisque .... *(Higher)*

d car .... i même si .... n en plus ....

e donc .... j ou .... o ne...ni ....

2 Fill in the gaps with the correct conjunction chosen from the three options in **bold**.

a Je veux aller au parc, ... il pleut. **ou / par exemple / mais**

b Il se relaxe .... il va aller à la fête. **cependant / ensuite / puis**

c Je ne peux pas sortir .... je suis malade. **ou / mais / parce que**

d Sylvie parle .... ma sœur. **car / comme / même si**

e Tu peux venir ce soir, ... tu veux. **si / et / par contre**

f J'aime mon frère .... il est très sympa. **puis / par exemple / car**

3 Circle the correct conjunction to complete the sentences below.

a Je voudrais courir ce soir, **puis** / **mais** j'ai mal à la tête.

b Ta famille est sympa — **si** / **par exemple** ton père est drôle.

c **Si** / **Ou** tu manges le gâteau, je vais être triste.

d Je me lève **cependant** / **et** je prends mon petit-déjeuner.

4 Choose the correct form of **à** or **de** from the box to complete the sentences.

a Je viens .... France et tu viens .... Québec.

b Je vais donner des cadeaux .... enfants .... école.

c On peut changer de l'argent .... banque ou .... poste.

d Pierre joue .... foot le samedi mais moi, je vais .... piscine.

e Est-ce que tu te souviens .... chien .... supermarché ?

f Est-ce qu'il y a .... légumes ou .... viande dans le repas ?

| au |
| à la |
| à l' |
| aux |
| de |
| du |
| de la |
| des |

Section Thirteen — Nouns, Articles and Linking Words

5 Translate these sentences into **English**.

a Elle va aller en vacances pendant un mois.

....

b Pendant l'année scolaire, j'ai appris à jouer d'un instrument de musique.

....

c J'apprends le français depuis quatre ans.

....

d J'ai pris une photo devant le pont avant de le traverser.

....

e J'ai parlé avec mon père en préparant le repas.

....

6 Choose the French word from the box to replace the English prepositions underlined below.

a The dog is under the table. ....

b Your bag is on the chair. ....

c I left the house without my keys. ....

d I'm going swimming after school. ....

e I had lunch at Juliette's. ....

f I went to the cinema with my friends. ....

g I arrived before you. ....

| chez |
| avant |
| sous |
| après |
| avec |
| sans |
| sur |

7 Translate these sentences into **French** using the prepositions in **bold**.

Don't forget that 'de + le' becomes 'du'.

a The school is situated between the swimming pool and the library.   **entre**

....

b There is a shopping centre in front of the train station.   **devant**

....

c There is a supermarket next to the park.   **à côté de**

....

Section Thirteen — Nouns, Articles and Linking Words

Adjectives

1 Underline all of the adjectives in the sentences below.

- **a** L'examen était facile.
- **b** Tes amis sont amusants.
- **c** Thomas a un vieux chien.
- **d** C'est une belle histoire.
- **e** Le nouveau film est triste.
- **f** Alice habite dans une grande maison.
- **g** J'ai une bonne idée.
- **h** Le voyage est long et ennuyeux.

2 Cross out the incorrect form of the adjectives in **bold** to complete these sentences.

- **a** Isabelle a les yeux **bleu** / **bleus**.
- **b** J'habite dans un appartement **moderne** / **modernes**.
- **c** La **premier** / **première** question est très **difficile** / **difficiles**.
- **d** Susanna porte un uniforme **rouge** / **rouges**, mais mon pantalon est **noir** / **noire**.
- **e** Mes frères sont assez **sportifs** / **sportives**.
- **f** L'animal est **vieux** / **vieille** et **heureux** / **heureuse**.

3 Fill in the gaps in these sentences using the correct form of the adjectives in **bold**.

- **a** Elle a un sac .... **blanc**
- **b** Il travail pour une entreprise .... **étranger**
- **c** Florence et Charlotte sont les .... à arriver. **dernier**
- **d** Ce portable est trop .... **cher**
- **e** Ma chambre d'hôtel est .... **propre**

4 Using the word **vert** with the correct endings, translate these phrases into **French**.

- **a** the green mountain
- **b** the green eyes
- **c** the green space
- **d** the green book
- **e** the green houses
- **f** the green tree

5 Translate the sentences below into **French**. The adjectives you should use are in **bold**, but you'll need to change them into the correct form.

a My parents are crazy. **fou**

....

b The old house is very beautiful. **vieux, beau**

....

c Your aunt is interesting. **intéressant**

....

d The film was rubbish and the story was boring. **nul, ennuyeux**

....

6 Complete the table of possessive adjectives below.

	My	Your (inf., sing.)	His / her / its	Our	Your (formal, pl.)	Their
Masculine singular		ton			votre	
Feminine singular			sa	notre		
Plural	mes					leurs

7 Cross out the incorrect demonstrative adjective in **bold** to complete these sentences.

a Je pense que **ce / cette** travail est un peu ennuyeux.

b **Cet / Ce** hôpital est excellent.

c **Ces / Cette** enfants sont timides.

d Je vais aller dans les Alpes **cet / cette** année.

8 Rewrite each of these sentences, replacing the English word in brackets with the correct indefinite adjective in **French**.

a Je joue au foot (**each**) week-end. ....

b Eric a acheté (**some**) légumes. ....

c Je peux chanter (**several**) chansons. ....

d (**None**) de mes amis ne nage. ....

Adverbs, Quantifiers and Intensifiers

1 Turn each of these adjectives into adverbs.

a facile ....

b récent ....

c parfait ....

d rapide ....

e égal ....

f seul ....

2 Fill in the gaps in these sentences using the correct French translation of the adverbs in **bold**.

a Il court très .... donc il a perdu la course. **slowly**

b L'examen de maths était .... difficile. **really**

c Il travail .... pour réussir ses examens. **so much**

d ...., je me lève à sept heures. **Normally**

e À l'hôpital, elle parle .... au médecin. **calmly**

3 Underline the adverb in each of these sentences, and then translate the adverb into **English**.

a Malheureusement, ma sœur a oublié de t'appeler. ....

b Christophe a finalement terminé ses examens. ....

c Vous m'avez clairement aidé. ....

d Il parle fièrement de son succès. ....

e Elle n'est pas encore arrivée. ....

4 Translate these sentences into **French**, using the adverb formed from the adjective in brackets.

a He sings well. (**bon**) ....

b She plays badly. (**mauvais**) ....

c He arrived quickly. (**rapide**) ....

5 Choose the French adverb from the box that matches the English adverb in **bold** to complete each sentence.

a ...., nous avons visité la tour. **yesterday**

b La campagne est .... calme. **very**

c ...., il mange à huit heures. **sometimes**

d Ils vont voyager .... **tomorrow**

e Ton cadeau est .... arrivé. **already**

très
déjà
hier
demain
parfois

6 Translate each of these adverbial phrases into **English**.

a en général ....

b par exemple ....

c tous les jours ....

d en retard ....

e en même temps ....

f de temps en temps ....

g la semaine dernière ....

h l'année prochaine ....

7 Use a French adverb to fill the gap in each of these sentences and match the English translation.

a Je l'ai vu .... *I saw it over there.*

b C'est mon anniversaire .... *It's my birthday today.*

c Mon père a laissé ses vêtements .... *My dad has left his clothes everywhere.*

d L'aéroport est assez .... de la ville. *The airport is quite far from the town.*

e Venez ...., s'il vous plaît. *Come here, please.*

8 Translate the sentences below into **French**.

a André reads the newspaper every day.

....

b She has a bit of time.

....

c I waited patiently for the results.

....

Comparatives and Superlatives

1 Complete these comparative sentences. Remember to add any necessary agreements.

Example Jean est **grand**, mais Chantelle est .... *plus grande que Jean.*

a Sofia est **sérieuse**, mais Amir est ....

b Le roman est **intéressant**, mais les films sont ....

c Marc est **fort** mais Rose est ....

2 Complete the table below using Arnaud's description of his family. Some of the answers have been filled in already.

> J'ai un frère qui s'appelle David, et une sœur qui s'appelle Julia. Je suis assez intelligent, mais David est plus intelligent que moi, et Julia est encore plus intelligente que David. David n'est pas aussi embêtant que Julia, et je suis moins embêtant que David. David est plus grand que moi, et Julia est plus petite que moi. Julia est plus sportive que moi, et David est moins sportif que moi. David est plus gentil que Julia et je suis plus méchant que Julia.

	Least	Middle	Most
intelligent	Arnaud		
annoying		David	
tall	Julia		
sporty			Julia
kind			

3 Translate these sentences into **French** using **le plus, la plus** or **les plus**.

a This play is the most exciting. ....

b I am funny, but he is the funniest. ....

c These flowers are the prettiest. ....

4 Cross out the incorrect comparative or superlative adverbs in **bold** to complete these sentences.

a Tous les gâteaux sont bons, mais les gâteaux au chocolat sont **les meilleurs** / **les meilleures**.

b Le foot est **pire que** / **le pire que** le rugby.

c C'est en ville que la qualité de l'air est **la pire** / **le pire**.

d Mes notes ont été **meilleure que** / **meilleures que** l'année dernière.

5 Turn the adjectives and adverbs below into comparatives and superlatives.

	bon	mauvais	bien	mal
Comparative				
Superlative	le meilleur			

6 Underline the comparatives and translate them into **English**. The first one has been done as an example.

Example Michelle recycle <u>plus qu'</u>Ahmed. .... *more than* ....

a Pierre court aussi vite que Nadim. ....

b Tu joues au tennis moins souvent que Fred. ....

c Sam mange plus tôt que Laura. ....

7 Cross out the incorrect comparative adverb to complete these sentences. Then translate the sentences into **English**.

a La situation est **pire** / **plus mal** que ce matin.

....

b Matthieu travaille **meilleur** / **mieux** à l'école que Charles.

....

8 Translate these sentences into **French**.

a I travel less often than you.

....

b Henry plays video games better than all of his friends.

....

c She dances the best.

....

d My mum goes to the market the most regularly.

....

Present Tense

1 Underline the verbs in each sentence.

a   Je vais en Suisse la semaine prochaine.
b   J'aime les fruits et les légumes.
c   C'est encore une journée de pluie.
d   Tu vois ta tante le dimanche.
e   Je préfère les films d'action.
f   J'ai deux petits frères.
g   Vous faites vos devoirs.
h   Le mercredi, il mange seulement du fromage.
i   Nous détestons le sport et la physique.
j   Il y a des élèves très bavards dans ma classe.

2 Write out the correct form of each verb in the present tense, matching the person given.

a   manger — il   ....
b   donner — nous   ....
c   acheter — vous   ....
d   finir — je   ....
e   choisir — ils   ....
f   partager — vous   ....
g   supporter — elles   ....
h   suivre — tu   ....
i   cacher — on   ....
j   attendre — vous   ....
k   remplir — elle   ....
l   vendre — je   ....

3 Complete the sentences by adding the correct verb endings in the present tense.

a   Il rest…… à la maison parce qu'il regard…… le match de foot à la télé.

b   Nous habit…… dans un appartement au bord de la mer et vous pouv…… venir chez vous.

c   Je mang…… chez moi tous les jours à midi, mais mes amis mang…… au café.

d   Vous parl…… à votre amie au téléphone, et elle vous parl…… de ses vacances.

4 Translate these sentences into **French**.

a   We're running in the park.

b   You ('tu') are playing football.

c   They study every day.

d   I'm taking photos.

e   He's writing a story.

f   You ('vous') are leaving today.

5 Write in the present tense forms of the verb **être** — to be.

- **a** je ....
- **b** tu ....
- **c** il / elle / on ....
- **d** nous ....
- **e** vous ....
- **f** ils / elles ....

6 Write in the present tense forms of the verb **avoir** — to have.

- **a** j' ....
- **b** tu ....
- **c** il / elle / on ....
- **d** nous ....
- **e** vous ....
- **f** ils / elles ....

7 Write in the present tense forms of the verbs below. Some are irregular.

- **a** je .... **faire**
- **b** tu .... **aller**
- **c** il / elle / on .... **vouloir**
- **d** nous .... **devoir**
- **e** vous .... **faire**
- **f** il / elle / on .... **faire**
- **g** nous .... **aller**
- **h** vous .... **vouloir**
- **i** ils / elles .... **devoir**
- **j** je .... **savoir**

8 Fill in the gaps with the right form of the verb in **bold**.

- **a** Il .... du thé. **boire**
- **b** Ils .... toujours ça. **dire**
- **c** Je .... un journal. **lire**
- **d** Est-ce que vous .... danser ? **savoir**
- **e** Elles .... beaucoup de photos. **prendre**
- **f** Vous .... la porte. **ouvrir**
- **g** Est-ce que tu .... venir avec moi au cinéma ? **vouloir**
- **h** Elle .... faire ses devoirs. **devoir**
- **i** Nous .... faire une promenade s'il fait beau. **pouvoir**

Past Tenses

1 Write in the past participles of these regular verbs.

a	acheter	....	**g**	entendre	....
b	danser	....	**h**	venir	....
c	dormir	....	**i**	finir	....
d	cacher	....	**j**	jouer	....
e	manger	....	**k**	vendre	....
f	prendre	....	**l**	choisir	....

2 Complete these sentences by adding the correct form of **avoir**.

a Ma belle-mère m'.................................. donné de beaux cadeaux.

b Nous .... célébré l'anniversaire de mon père.

c Tu .... porté un nouveau pantalon.

d Mes cousins .... mangé des frites.

e Vous .... trouvé un métier intéressant.

3 Fill in the gaps with the perfect tense of the irregular verb in **bold**.

a Tu .... le repas sur la table. **mettre**

b Il .... le premier roman de son auteur préféré. **lire**

c Les parents .... une lettre à leurs enfants. **écrire**

d Vous .... l'article en Français. **traduire**

4 Fill in the perfect tense forms of the verbs in **bold**. They all take **être**.

a Elle .... après le concours. **partir**

b Il .... me voir samedi après-midi. **venir**

c Mon petit frère .... malade à l'école. **tomber**

d Nous *(fem.)* .... dans la salle de classe. **entrer**

e Ils .... ici pendant les vacances. **rester**

f Je *(fem.)* .... au collège en septembre. **rentrer**

Section Fifteen — Verbs and Tenses

5 Write the correct form of **faire** in the imperfect tense.

a Tu .... des gâteaux pour moi.

b Je .... du vélo tous les matins.

c Qu'est-ce qu'elles .... hier soir ?

d Nous .... beaucoup de devoirs tous les jours.

6 Write the correct form of **avoir** in the imperfect tense.

a On .... toujours quelque chose à faire.

b J'........................... trois leçons par semaine.

c Vous .... mon adresse.

d Ils .... des problèmes.

7 Write the correct form of **être** in the imperfect tense.

a Tu .... très content de recevoir le prix.

b J'........................... toujours en retard.

c Vous .... très jeunes en 2006.

d Les films .... assez amusants.

8 Translate the sentences below into **English**. Write them all as 'was / were ...ing'.

a Je regardais la télévision. ....

b On attendait le facteur. ....

c Il chantait dans son bain. ....

9 Translate the sentences below into **French**.

a I used to play football. ....

b You ('tu') used to go to the park. ....

c She used to buy the newspaper. ....

10 Translate the sentence below into **English**.

J'habite en Angleterre depuis 2007.

....

Talking about the Future & The Conditional

1. Give the immediate future tense forms of these verbs, matching the person given.

   The immediate future is formed with the present tense of 'aller' + an infinitive.

   Example choisir — je .... *je vais choisir* ....

   a manger — tu ....

   b finir — nous ....

   c commencer — ils ....

   d prendre — vous ....

   e aller — elles ....

2. Change these sentences from the past or present tense to the immediate future tense in **French**.

   a Je lis les articles en ligne. ....

   b Elles ont voyagé en Europe. ....

   c Tu organisais une grande fête. ....

   d On prépare le repas tôt. ....

3. Give the proper future tense forms of these verbs.

   Example arriver — vous .... *vous arriverez* ....

   a avoir — je ....

   b être — elle ....

   c danser — on ....

   d jouer — nous ....

   e faire — tu ....

4. Write in the proper future tense forms of the verbs in **bold**.

   Example Demain, nous .... *achèterons* .... une voiture.   **buy**

   a Tu .... les lettres.   **forget**

   b On .... un film très triste.   **watch**

   c Elle .... au supermarché demain.   **go**

   d Vous .... la carte au restaurant.   **ask**

Section Fifteen — Verbs and Tenses

5 Complete the sentences with the correct conditional form of **vouloir**.

a   Je .... une boisson, s'il vous plaît.

b   Tu .... payer le vendeur.

c   Elle .... rentrer à la maison.

d   Il .... voir le concours.

e   Est-ce que tu .... du thé ou du café ?

6 Put the verbs in **bold** into the correct conditional form.

a	Je .... rester chez moi.		**préférer**
b	Il .... manger le gâteau entier.		**aimer**
c	Nous .... voir un match de foot.		**détester**
d	Je .... au basket si je n'avais pas mal à la jambe.		**jouer**
e	Ils ont dit qu'ils .... en train cet après-midi.		**voyager**
f	Je le .... si c'était moins difficile.		**faire**
g	Ils .... toute la nuit.		**danser**
h	J'........................ au cinéma si j'avais le temps.		**aller**
i	Je .... heureux de vous voir.		**être**
j	Si je n'étais pas malade, j'........................ du vin.		**avoir**

7 Translate these sentences into **French**.

a   I would like to go to France to study.

   ....

b   You ('vous') would buy every bag in the shop.

   ....

c   She would watch the film with me.

   ....

d   We would like to help.

   ....

Reflexives, Negative Forms & Giving Orders

1 Fill in the reflexive pronoun for each person.

a   je .... lave

b   tu .... laves

c   il / elle .... lave

d   nous .... lavons

e   vous .... lavez

f   ils / elles .... lavent

2 Choose the right verb from the box, then use the present tense form of the verb to fill in the gap.

Example   Je .... *m'excuse* .... — j'ai perdu votre portable.

a   On .... toujours à l'eau chaude.

b   Tu .... de mon anniversaire ?

c   L'appartement .... de l'autre côté du supermarché.

d   S'il n'a pas de carte, il .... toujours.

e   Je ne .... jamais avant sept heures du matin.

> se souvenir
> se lever
> se laver
> se perdre
> se trouver
> ~~s'excuser~~

3 Add any missing agreements to these reflexive verbs in the present tense.

a   Ce matin, elle s'est levé............. à huit heures.

b   Le couple s'est quitté............. après les vacances.

c   Il s'est lavé............. trois fois après le match.

d   Elles se sont preparé............. ensemble avant la fête.

e   Nous (*m*) nous sommes organisé............. pour le festival.

4 Make these sentences negative by adding **ne...pas**.

a   Je mange du fromage. ....

b   Nous lavons nos vêtements. ....

c   C'est loin d'ici. ....

d   Il lit des livres. ....

e   C'est la même chose. ....

f   J'ai des billets. ....

Section Fifteen — Verbs and Tenses

5 Make these sentences negative, using the words in brackets.

a Il a visité le château. (pas) ....

b Ils vont au théâtre. (jamais) ....

c Je suis allée au collège. (jamais) ....

d Il a compris. (rien) ....

H e Tout le monde a mangé du poisson. (personne) ....

6 Translate these sentences into **French**.

a I haven't watched the new film yet.

....

b She only has one hour to finish the exam.

....

c I'm not going to eat meat anymore.

....

d The hotel is neither pretty nor clean.

....

7 Put the missing verb into the French sentences. They all need to be in the imperative form.

a .... tes devoirs ! — *Finish your homework!*

b Francine et Agnès, ... avec nous! — *Francine and Agnès, come with us!*

c .... tes légumes ! — *Eat your vegetables!*

d .... encore une fois ! — *Try once more! (to a friend)*

e .... plus positif ! — *Be more positive! (to a friend)*

f .... gentils ! — *Be kind! (to a group of children)*

g .... au marché ! — *Let's go to the market!*

h .... un gâteau ! — *Let's make a cake!*

Section Fifteen — Verbs and Tenses

-ing Verbs, Impersonal Verbs & the Passive

1 Turn the infinitives below into present participles.

Example vouloir ....*voulant*....

a donner ....
b partir ....
c entendre ....
d acheter ....
e choisir ....
f perdre ....
g faire ....
h aller ....
i être ....

2 Complete the sentences by changing the infinitives into present participles. Then translate the sentences into English.

a J'ai joué du piano en .... **parler**

....

b En .... dans la cuisine, je vois mon père. **entrer**

....

c Nous avons expliqué la situation en .... **marcher**

....

d Elle est entrée en .... **rire**

....

e Il a crié en .... **tomber**

....

3 Translate these sentences into **French**.

a After having made bread, I ate it.

....

b After having left, he came back.

....

Section Fifteen — Verbs and Tenses

4 Match up the French sentences with the English translations.

a   Il faut chanter très vite. ....   1.   It's nice at the beach.

b   Il fait beau à la plage. ....   2.   You must go out with her.

c   Il fait froid aujourd'hui. ....   3.   There is a lot of snow.

d   Il y a beaucoup de neige. ....   4.   It's cold today.

e   Il faut sortir avec elle. ....   5.   It is necessary to sing very quickly.

5 Match up the French sentences with the English translations.

a   Il est difficile de dire. ....   1.   It's important to eat well.

b   Il vaut la peine d'acheter un billet. ....   2.   Some details are missing.

c   Il vaut mieux tard que jamais. ....   3.   It is difficult to say.

d   Il manque des détails. ....   4.   It's worth buying a ticket.

e   Il est important de bien manger. ....   5.   It's better late than never.

6 Translate the underlined words into **English**.

a   <u>L'animal est lavé</u> par l'homme. ....

b   <u>Je suis regardé</u> par tout le monde au théâtre. ....

c   <u>Les lettres sont envoyées</u> par leur mère. ....

d   <u>Vous êtes trouvé</u> par la police. ....

e   <u>On a fermé la route</u> après l'accident. ....

7 Change these sentences from the **French active** to the **French passive**.

a   Beaucoup de gens préparent le repas.

   ....

b   Marc ne mange pas la nourriture

   ....

c   Les enfants aiment mes histoires.

   ....

d   Mon frère écrit la chanson.

   ....

Answers

The answers to the translation questions are sample answers only, just to give you an idea of one way to translate them. There may be different ways to translate these sentences that are also correct.

For dictation and translation questions, this symbol (|) shows where to divide the marks. There is 1 mark awarded for the first part of the text, and 1 mark awarded for the second.

Section One — General Stuff

Pages 2-3: Numbers, Times, Days and Dates
1) a) 3   b) 8   c) €156   d) 16   e) around ten
2) a) B   b) C   c) C
3) a) D   b) B   c) E
4) a) Il est né | le dix avril.
   b) J'ai acheté | quatorze melons.
   c) Il est | dix-huit heures.
   d) Je trouve l'été | splendide.

Pages 4-5: Questions and Being Polite
1) a) C   b) D   c) A
2) a) Bienvenue au | château royal.
   b) Félicitations pour | ton succès à l'examen.
   c) Attention | à la route.
   d) Voici la porte | d'entrée.
3) a) avons   b) tu   c) désolée
4) a) Pourquoi arrives-tu | en retard le jeudi ?
   b) Où va le professeur d'histoire | pour ses vacances ?
   c) Combien coûtent | ces légumes frais ?
   d) Est-ce que tu aimes nager | dans les lacs de montagne ?

Pages 6-7: Opinions
1) a) P+N   b) N   c) P   d) P
2) a) favourite singer.
   b) Sabrina doesn't write her own songs.
   c) extraordinary.
   d) earn money.
4) a) A   b) B   c) A   d) B

Section Two — Identity and Relationships with Others

Pages 8-9: About Yourself and My Family & Friends
1) Here are some examples of sentences you could have written:
   C'est un couple gay.
   Le couple a un enfant.
   C'est une famille heureuse.
2) a) I was born in England, | but my family is German.
   b) He speaks | French and Spanish.
   c) I have a father, a step-mother | and lots of brothers and sisters.
   d) I love spending time with my cousins. | We chat often.
   e) She does not get on well | with her aunt and uncle.
4) a) Je suis née dans | un pays européen.
   b) J'ai une vie de famille | très heureuse.
   c) Ma maman est gentille. | Elle aide toujours les autres.
   d) Mes parents | me manquent beaucoup.

Pages 10-11: Describing People and Relationships
1) a) L'enfant de mon frère | ressemble à notre père.
   b) Ils sont très fiers | d'être travailleurs.
   c) L'homme et la femme | se disputent beaucoup.
   d) La communication et la confiance | sont très importantes.
   e) Mon oncle | était célibataire.
3) a) sensitive
   b) Her last boyfriend cheated on her.
   c) He would not smoke.
      He would not be lazy.
   d) national parks
4) a) She wants to be independent.
   b) His girlfriend isn't ready to get married.

Section Three — Healthy Living and Lifestyle

Pages 12-13: Food and Healthy & Unhealthy Living
1) a) C   b) A   c) D
3) a) I think that | he is quite active.
   b) My mother doesn't drink alcohol | and doesn't smoke.
   c) Normally, I do a lot of sport | to stay in shape.
   d) I'm going to go to | the swimming pool tomorrow.
   e) Last night, I prepared | a balanced meal for my family.

Pages 14-15: Illnesses and Treatments
1) a) prendre   b) tombé   c) à la
2) a) B   b) A   c) B
3) a) a car accident
   b) stay at home for two weeks / avoid sports activities
   c) hands
      back
4) a) Mon copain a mal | à la jambe.
   b) Il est | très fatigué.
   c) Demain il va aller | à l'hôpital.
   d) Il veut changer | de médicaments.

Section Four — Education

Pages 16-17: School Subjects and School Life
2) a) A   b) C   c) A
3) a) P+N   b) P   c) N   d) N   e) P+N

Pages 18-19: School Pressures and Difficulties
1) a) A and B   b) D and E
2) a) The school requires us | to wear a school uniform.
   b) According to me, behaviour is | the biggest problem at school.
   c) Unfortunately, I made a mistake | in the English test.
   d) The teacher will correct | my homework during breaktime.
   e) The headteacher doesn't allow | pupils to use their phones.
4) a) Je m'inquiète pour | l'examen de géographie mardi.
   b) Les notes de mon ami(e) | sont toujours géniales.
   c) Je pense que les règles au lycée | sont assez strictes.
   d) Porter un pantalon vert à l'école | est interdit.
   e) Souvent, j'aide les autres étudiants | avec leurs devoirs.

Section Five — Future Study and Work

Pages 20-21: Education Post-16 and Career Choices

1) a) go to university
   b) Her teacher said she wasn't ready.
   c) to improve her practical skills
      to earn money
2) a) D b) E c) B d) A
4) a) M b) N c) S d) Y

Theme 1 — Mixed Practice

Pages 22-24: Mixed Practice — Foundation

1) Here are some examples of sentences you could have written:
   Une élève essaie de travailler.
   La fille est très travailleuse.
   L'élève suit les règles.
   Il y a des tables.
   Un garçon jette une chaise.
2) a) affreuse
   b) apporté
   c) la
   d) deviennent
   e) heureux
4) a) After the accident, | I had a headache.
   b) My mum | fell yesterday.
   c) Tomorrow, I will organise | a meeting.
   d) There is a medical emergency | at the hospital.
   e) The doctor always finds | a solution to the problem.
5) a) P b) N c) P + N d) P
6) a) J'ai | une sœur.
   b) Elle s'entend bien | avec nos parents.
   c) Il y a beaucoup de | générations différentes dans ma famille.
   d) L'année dernière, j'ai rencontré | mon partenaire à une fête.
   e) J'espère | me marier un jour.

Pages 25-27: Mixed Practice — Both Tiers

1) a) A and B b) C and D c) A and D
2) a) M b) C c) L d) M e) L
3) a) Mon frère | est petit.
   b) Elle avait les cheveux noirs | et les yeux marron.
   c) Je ressemble beaucoup à | ma mère.
   d) Je respecte toujours | mon oncle italien.
5) a) N b) P c) P + N d) N
6) a) disgusting.
      it can cause health problems.
   b) relax.
      smoke less often.
   c) she stopped (last year).
      smoking is really bad for your health.

Pages 28-31: Mixed Practice — Higher

1) a) Il travaille pour | un établissement indépendant.
   b) La concurrence est énorme | dans ce secteur.
   c) Je veux créer | de nouvelles lois.
   d) Je suis prête pour | la prochaine étape.
4) a) when he was in Year 10
   b) his teacher inspired him
   c) the number of tests
      nasty students
6) a) Yesterday, my teacher advised me | to think about my future career.
   b) I will take a gap year | before enrolling in university.
   c) In the future, she wants to be | a researcher or a scientist.
   d) The development of trade is | very important for the economy.
   e) According to a survey, most | young people cannot find a job.
9) a) a career change.
   b) take a gap year.
   c) learn new skills.
   d) research.

Section Six — Free-time Activities

Pages 32-33: Music, Cinema, Theatre and TV

2) a) Saturday evening
   b) action film
   c) They got the time wrong.
   d) The actors were bad.
3) a) B b) B
4) a) Je regarde la télé parce que | je pense que c'est passionnant.
   b) Il voudrait apprendre à | jouer d'un instrument.
   c) Ma sœur téléchargeait | des chansons sur Internet.
   d) Ils aiment la plupart des genres de musique, | mais ils n'aiment pas la musique pop.
   e) Je m'intéresse aux | effets spéciaux qu'on utilise sur scène.

Pages 34-35: Sport, Going Out and Other Hobbies

1) a) I like doing | sport and exercise.
   b) My mum is | very active.
   c) After school, I am going to go | to the swimming pool at the sports centre.
   d) I'm going to take part | in a race soon.
   e) Swimming is good | for my health.
3) a) He had to wait for a long time to get a table.
      The waiter was lazy.
   b) He couldn't stand / bear the noise.
   c) The food was cold.
      The meal was too expensive.
4) Here are some examples of sentences you could have written:
   Les filles ont gagné un match.
   Elles jouent au foot.
   Elles sont une équipe.
   L'équipe est heureuse.
   Elles célèbrent un but.

Section Seven — Customs, Festivals and Celebrations

Pages 36-37: Customs, Festivals and Celebrations

2) a) C b) B c) C
3) a) sport(s) / sporting activities
      a show
   b) She thinks it's the best festival of the year. /
      She loves going there every summer.
   c) (more or less) every genre
   d) all over the world

Section Eight — Celebrity Culture

Pages 38-39: Favourite Celebrities & Celebrity Life
2) a) Je ne veux pas | être célèbre.
   b) L'auteur vend | des millions de livres.
   c) Je m'inspire de | plusieurs acteurs formidables.
   d) Les célébrités créent | leurs propres marques.
3) a) C   b) B   c) C

Theme 2 — Mixed Practice

Pages 40-42: Mixed Practice — Foundation
2) a) B   b) D   c) C
3) a) I go swimming | on Mondays.
   b) It's my dream to learn | to play an instrument.
   c) This weekend, we are going | to go to a festival.
   d) Every evening, | I listen to my favourite singer.
   e) Yesterday, it was a public holiday, | so I went to the beach.
5) a) C   b) T   c) Y   d) C   e) T
6) a) N   b) P + N   c) N   d) P

Pages 43-46: Mixed Practice — Both Tiers
1) a) Mon frère | est très sportif.
   b) Je n'aime pas | regarder la télé.
   c) Je vais réserver | une table pour deux.
   d) On joue dans | une petite équipe locale.
3) a) Je n'aime pas regarder la télé. | Je préfère aller au théâtre.
   b) Il y a beaucoup d'acteurs célèbres | dans ce nouveau film d'action.
   c) J'aime la politique internationale | donc je lis les journaux.
   d) Mon auteur préféré a écrit | un nouveau livre.
4) a) They share a special meal.
      Everyone wears nice clothes.
   b) B and D
5) a) Mon copain va | au temple chaque semaine.
   b) J'adore célébrer | la Saint-Valentin.
   c) J'ai toujours eu | une foi profonde.
   d) N'oubliez pas d'apporter | du jus de fruits.
7) a) every year
   b) in the south of the island
      by the sea
   c) more than 24 hours
   d) C
8) a) she was excellent in her latest film.
   b) on a Mediterranean island.
   c) write some new songs.
      do some international concerts.

Pages 47-49: Mixed Practice — Higher
1) a) to learn to play a musical instrument
   b) transport
      accommodation
   c) Any two from:
   • spend time with Diane
   • watch a football match at Wembley stadium
   • eat at a famous chef's restaurant
4) a) Tu veux aller | au restaurant français.
   b) J'ai gagné un concours national | avec ma nouvelle chanson.
   c) Ses photos encouragent les gens | à être plus positifs.
   d) Elle poste souvent des vidéos | de son travail sur les réseaux sociaux.
   e) Cette semaine, j'organiserai un événement | pour célébrer le succès d'un artiste local.

5) a) F   b) P   c) N   d) P   e) N
6) a) the development of modern medicine.
   b) some surprising scenes.
   c) a war on another planet (in 2150).
   d) the special effects.

Section Nine — Travel and Tourism

Pages 50-51: Where to Go, Accommodation and Travel
2) a) C and D   b) B and D   c) A and B
3) a) They think it's too expensive to go alone.
   b) waiter
   c) You can learn another language.
      You can earn a bit of money.

Pages 52-53: What to Do
1) a) F   b) D   c) L
2) a) J'achète | une pomme.
   b) La grotte ferme | à seize heures.
   c) Il y a beaucoup | de touristes.
   d) L'entrée du château | n'est pas ici.
4) a) Je profite de mes vacances | à l'étranger chaque année.
   b) Cet après-midi, je nagerai | dans le lac calme près de notre hôtel.
   c) Ma mère a commandé | une boisson et une glace.
   d) Il a décidé de m'accompagner | au marché.
   e) L'ancienne gare centrale | est maintenant un musée d'art moderne.

Section Ten — Media and Technology

Pages 54-55: Technology and The Internet
1) a) you can discover new things online.
      learn Spanish.
   b) spend too much time in front of a screen.
      the influence of advertising online.
2) a) N   b) P + N   c) P   d) P + N
3) a) J'ai | un ordinateur portable.
   b) Je préfère acheter | des vêtements en ligne.
   c) Il y a beaucoup de jeux | et de films sur mon ordinateur.
   d) Je vais envoyer | l'e-mail demain.
   e) Hier, mon téléphone | ne marchait pas.

Pages 56-57: Social Media
1) a) at least four hours
   b) to watch lots of short videos
   c) spend time with her family or read more each night
      she sleeps better or she has less worries
2) a) T   b) J   c) A   d) T
3) Here are some examples of sentences you could have written:
   Il y a un groupe de quatre influenceurs.
   L'homme enregistre une vidéo.
   Les femmes ont deux ordinateurs.
   Il y a une table.
   Il y a des cafés sur la table.
4) a) C   b) B   c) B

Section Eleven — Where People Live

Pages 58-59: Where You Live and The Home
1) a) N b) P c) P + N d) N
2) a) in Canada
   b) to be nearer to her new job
   c) She lives alone.
   d) a garden
4) a) J'habite dans | une petite ville en Angleterre.
   b) La maison se situe | dans le sud de la France.
   c) Il y a trois chambres, | une belle cuisine et un jardin.
   d) J'habitais dans | la banlieue de la capitale.
   e) C'est mon rêve de construire | une maison à côté d'un lac.

Pages 60-61: The Local Area, Directions and Weather
2) a) to go to the supermarket
   b) Other supermarkets are too far from his home.
   c) The clothes are too expensive there.
   d) the exit
   e) Any two from:
      It's efficient to shop there.
      You can find everything.
      It's a good way to support the local economy.
3) a) The stadium is located | in front of the station.
   b) My friends tell me that | I live too far from the town.
   c) The climate is relatively warm | and it rains less often.
   d) According to the weather forecast, | there will be snow next week.
   e) When I was young, | I lived in the west of the region.

Section Twelve — Environmental and Social Issues

Pages 62-63: Protecting the Environment & Environmental Problems
1) a) It helps us to use fewer natural resources.
   b) Recycle their own rubbish.
      Buy fewer plastic products.
   c) boxes
      plastic bags
2) B and D
3) a) peut b) animaux

Pages 64-65: Social Issues
2) a) Il y a une manifestation | dans ma ville aujourd'hui.
   b) Les citoyens luttent pour défendre | l'égalité entre les hommes et les femmes.
   c) La semaine prochaine, j'organiserai | un débat sur la politique à l'école.
   d) Le niveau de violence dans les rues | a été un choc pour moi.
   e) Hier soir, le / la porte-parole du nouveau président | a annoncé sa victoire.
3) a) H b) Y c) I d) H e) Y
4) a) A b) C c) C

Theme 3 — Mixed Practice

Pages 66-69: Mixed Practice — Foundation
1) a) F b) F c) P d) N e) F
3) a) Quelle est votre adresse, | s'il vous plaît ?
   b) J'aime la campagne | parce que c'est calme.
   c) Nous sommes allé(e)s | au magasin de ma sœur hier.
   d) Il y a un manque de | bibliothèques dans ma ville.
   e) J'habite dans | le nord de l'Angleterre.
5) a) A and E   b) C and F
8) a) E b) A c) B
9) Here are some examples of sentences you could have written:
   Il y a un homme, une femme et une fille.
   Une famille utilise la téchnologie.
   La fille a un portable.
   Le père utilise un ordinateur.
   Ils ne parlent pas.

Pages 70-71: Mixed Practice — Both Tiers
1) a) C b) P c) E d) C e) P
2) a) Communication is not simple.
   b) You can discover new interests.
   c) learning a new language
      meeting people
3) a) Elle est arrivée | au port hier soir.
   b) Je n'aime pas | prendre l'avion.
   c) Notre retour était | vraiment stressant.
   d) Ils ne veulent pas | rentrer chez eux.

Pages 72-75: Mixed Practice — Higher
1) a) A castle
   b) A bus
   c) Any two from:
      A ticket costs five euros.
      There is a beautiful view of the countryside.
      You can't take photos inside the building.
2) a) F b) N c) P d) N e) F
3) a) A and B b) C and D c) B and D
5) a) Tunisia
   b) Europe
   c) London
   d) windy
6) a) Charge your phone — | I sent you a message.
   b) Protection against online attacks | is very important.
   c) The consumer can easily send back their purchase | if there's a problem.
   d) On social media, you can | like an image and add a comment.
   e) I broke my computer, | so I will buy a new device soon.
7) a) B b) C c) C d) A

Section Thirteen —
Nouns, Articles and Linking Words

Pages 76-77: Nouns and Articles
1) a) Elle aime manger des <u>fruits</u>.
   b) Le <u>professeur</u> a une nouvelle <u>voiture</u>.
   c) On parle <u>français</u> au <u>Canada</u>.
   d) J'ai reçu une <u>lettre</u> de <u>Sofiane</u>.
   e) Les <u>gens</u> dansent.
   f) C'est le <u>sac</u> de ma <u>mère</u>.
   g) <u>Manon</u> a acheté des <u>frites</u>.
   h) La <u>poste</u> est ouverte.
   i) Le <u>film</u> n'est pas amusant.
   j) <u>Marie</u> habite près de mon <u>frère</u>.
2) a) m b) m c) m d) f e) m f) m g) f h) m
   i) m j) m k) f l) f m) m n) m o) m p) m
3) a) les tableaux — pictures
   b) les parcs — parks
   c) les fils — sons
   d) les feux — fires
   e) les prix — prizes
   f) les lieux — places
   g) les journaux — newspapers
   h) les hommes — men
   i) les châteaux — castles
   j) les bureaux — desks
4) a) Il y a trois <u>rues</u> entre le stade et l'hôpital.
   b) Mes amis aiment faire du sport, mais je préfère jouer à des <u>jeux</u>.
   c) Je vais souvent au zoo car j'aime bien voir les <u>animaux</u>.
   d) Il faut manger des fruits et des <u>légumes</u> tous les jours.
   e) Je dois acheter des <u>cadeaux</u> pour ma famille.
5) a) <u>Les</u> filles aiment jouer au foot.
   b) Ce soir, <u>le</u> repas va être traditionnel.
   c) Fermez <u>la</u> porte, s'il vous plaît.
   d) Nous avons trouvé tous <u>les</u> sacs sous <u>la</u> table.
   e) <u>L'</u>hôtel est à côté de chez moi.
6) a) J'ai acheté <u>un</u> café, <u>un</u> gâteau et <u>une</u> boisson.
   b) Ma mère a <u>une</u> sœur et <u>un</u> cousin.
   c) Dans mon jardin, il y a <u>un</u> arbre, <u>un</u> pont et trois chaises.
7) a) Je vais à la plage.
   b) Il va visiter le Maroc.
   c) Elle a une tante et un oncle.
8) a) Sylvie a <u>des</u> cousins.
   b) Je n'ai pas <u>de</u> livre.
   c) Ils ont gagné <u>de l'</u>argent.
   d) Il prend <u>du</u> poisson.
   e) Elle mange beaucoup <u>de</u> fromage.
   f) Richard n'a pas <u>de</u> portable.
   g) Il me donne <u>de la</u> glace.
   h) Je veux <u>des</u> billets.
9) a) Je vais au Sénégal cette année.
   b) Il vient d'Angleterre.

Pages 78-79: Pronouns
1) a) Mon chien est malade. <u>Il</u> ne mange pas beaucoup.
   b) Leur tante est médecin. <u>Elle</u> travaille dans un hôpital.
   c) Mes sœurs aiment les festivals de musique. <u>Elles</u> ont acheté des billets.
   d) Ses parents sont en vacances. <u>Ils</u> vont rentrer à la maison la semaine prochaine.
2) a) Tu <u>lui</u> as donné de l'eau.
   b) Il <u>m'</u>a apporté ton cahier.
   c) Je <u>t'</u>ai déjà parlé.
   d) Nous <u>vous</u> avons tout expliqué.
   e) Elle <u>nous</u> a acheté un cadeau.
3) a) Il est sorti avec <u>moi</u>.
   b) Elles ont écrit la chanson pour <u>toi</u>.
   c) Ils le font <u>eux</u>-mêmes.
   d) Il y est allé <u>lui</u>-même.
4) a) Qui chante ?
   b) À quoi penses-tu ?
   c) Que fais-tu le weekend ?
   d) Qui peut m'aider avec cet exercice ?
5) a) Le garçon <u>qui</u> porte un uniforme est très travailleur.
   b) Le repas <u>que</u> tu as préparé était bon.
   c) C'est un homme <u>qui</u> aime le fromage.
   d) Le touriste <u>qu'</u>ils ont vu était célèbre.
   e) Les vêtements <u>qu'</u>elle achète sont extraordinaires.
   f) La personne <u>qui</u> m'a volé la voiture était vieille.
6) a) quelque chose
   b) tout
   c) quelqu'un
   d) tout le monde
   e) plusieurs
   f) chacun(e)
7) a) That doesn't interest me much.
   b) That makes me laugh.
   c) This can help us do the exercises.
8) a) J'adore la plage. On <u>y</u> va quand il fait beau.
   b) J'ai besoin de lait. Est-ce que tu peux m'<u>en</u> acheter ?
   c) Je voudrais visiter le musée mais tu <u>y</u> es déjà allée.
   d) As-tu du pain? Je n'<u>en</u> ai plus.

Pages 80-81: Conjunctions and Prepositions
1) a) then / so
   b) if / whether
   c) but
   d) because / for
   e) so / therefore
   f) next
   g) like / as
   h) however
   i) even if
   j) or
   k) for example
   l) because
   m) as / because
   n) in addition / also
   o) neither...nor
2) a) Je veux aller au parc, <u>mais</u> il pleut.
   b) Il se relaxe <u>puis</u> il va aller à la fête.
   c) Je ne peux pas sortir <u>parce que</u> je suis malade.
   d) Sylvie parle <u>comme</u> ma sœur.
   e) Tu peux venir ce soir, <u>si</u> tu veux.
   f) J'aime mon frère <u>car</u> il est très sympa.
3) a) Je voudrais courir ce soir, <u>mais</u> j'ai mal à la tête.
   b) Ta famille est sympa, <u>par exemple</u> ton père est drôle.
   c) <u>Si</u> tu manges le gâteau, je vais être triste.
   d) Je me lève <u>et</u> je prends mon petit-déjeuner.
4) a) Je viens <u>de</u> France et tu viens <u>du</u> Québec.
   b) Je vais donner des cadeaux <u>aux</u> enfants <u>à l'</u>école.
   c) On peut changer de l'argent <u>à la</u> banque ou <u>à la</u> poste.
   d) Pierre joue <u>au</u> foot le samedi mais moi, je vais <u>à la</u> piscine.
   e) Est-ce que tu te souviens <u>du</u> chien <u>au</u> supermarché ?
   f) Est-ce qu'il y a <u>des</u> légumes ou <u>de la</u> viande dans le repas ?
5) a) She is going to go on holiday for a month.
   b) During the school year, I learnt to play a musical instrument.
   c) I've been learning French for four years.
   d) I took a photo in front of the bridge before crossing it.
   e) I talked to my father while preparing the meal.
6) a) sous
   b) sur
   c) sans
   d) après
   e) chez
   f) avec
   g) avant
7) a) L'école se trouve entre la piscine et la bibliothèque.
   b) Il y a un centre commercial devant la gare.
   c) Il y a un supermarché à côté du parc.

Section Fourteen — Adjectives and Adverbs

Pages 82-83: Adjectives
1) a) L'examen était <u>facile</u>.
   b) Tes amis sont <u>amusants</u>.
   c) Thomas a un <u>vieux</u> chien.
   d) C'est une <u>belle</u> histoire.
   e) Le <u>nouveau</u> film est <u>triste</u>.
   f) Alice habite dans une <u>grande</u> maison.
   g) J'ai une <u>bonne</u> idée.
   h) Le voyage est <u>long</u> et <u>ennuyeux</u>.
2) a) Isabelle a les yeux <u>bleus</u>.
   b) J'habite dans un appartement <u>moderne</u>.
   c) La <u>première</u> question est très <u>difficile</u>.
   d) Susanna porte un uniforme <u>rouge</u>, mais mon pantalon est <u>noir</u>.
   e) Mes frères sont assez <u>sportifs</u>.
   f) L'animal est <u>vieux</u> et <u>heureux</u>.
3) a) Elle a un sac <u>blanc</u>.
   b) Il travail pour une entreprise <u>étrangère</u>.
   c) Florence et Charlotte sont les <u>dernières</u> à arriver.
   d) Ce portable est trop <u>cher</u>.
   e) Ma chambre d'hôtel est <u>propre</u>.
4) a) la montagne verte
   b) les yeux verts
   c) l'espace vert
   d) le livre vert
   e) les maisons vertes
   f) l'arbre vert
5) a) Mes parents sont <u>fous</u>.
   b) La <u>vieille</u> maison est très <u>belle</u>.
   c) Ta tante est <u>intéressante</u>.
   d) Le film était <u>nul</u> et l'histoire était <u>ennuyeuse</u>.
6)

	My	Your (inf., sing.)	His / her / its	Our	Your (formal, pl.)	Their
Masculine singular	mon	ton	son	notre	votre	leur
Feminine singular	ma	ta	sa	notre	votre	leur
Plural	mes	tes	ses	nos	vos	leurs

7) a) Je pense que <u>ce</u> travail est un peu ennuyeux.
   b) <u>Cet</u> hôpital est excellent.
   c) <u>Ces</u> enfants sont timides.
   d) Je vais aller dans les Alpes <u>cette</u> année.
8) a) Je joue au foot <u>chaque</u> week-end.
   b) Eric a acheté <u>quelques</u> légumes.
   c) Je peux chanter <u>plusieurs</u> chansons.
   d) <u>Aucun</u> de mes amis ne nage.

Pages 84-85: Adverbs, Quantifiers and Intensifiers

1) a) facilement
   b) récemment
   c) parfaitement
   d) rapidement
   e) également
   f) seulement

2) a) Il court très <u>lentement</u> donc il a perdu la course.
   b) L'examen de maths était <u>vraiment</u> difficile.
   c) Il travaille <u>tellement</u> pour réussir ses examens.
   d) <u>Normalement</u>, je me lève à sept heures.
   e) À l'hôpital, elle parle <u>calmement</u> au médecin.

3) a) Malheureusement — unfortunately
   b) finalement — finally
   c) clairement — clearly
   d) fièrement — proudly
   e) encore — yet

4) a) Il chante bien.
   b) Elle joue mal.
   c) Il est arrivé rapidement.

5) a) <u>Hier</u>, nous avons visité la tour.
   b) La campagne est <u>très</u> calme.
   c) <u>Parfois</u>, il mange à huit heures.
   d) Ils vont voyager <u>demain</u>.
   e) Ton cadeau est <u>déjà</u> arrivé.

6) a) in general
   b) for example
   c) every day
   d) late
   e) at the same time
   f) from time to time
   g) last week
   h) next year

7) a) Je l'ai vu <u>là-bas</u>.
   b) C'est mon anniversaire <u>aujourd'hui</u>.
   c) Mon père a laissé ses vêtements <u>partout</u>.
   d) L'aéroport est assez <u>loin</u> de la ville.
   e) Venez <u>ici</u>, s'il vous plaît.

8) a) André lit le journal tous les jours.
   b) Elle a un peu de temps.
   c) J'ai attendu patiemment les résultats.

Pages 86-87: Comparatives and Superlatives

1) a) ...plus sérieux que Sofia.
   b) ...plus intéressants que le roman.
   c) ...plus forte que Marc.

2)

	Least	Middle	Most
intelligent	Arnaud	David	Julia
annoying	Arnaud	David	Julia
tall	Julia	Arnaud	David
sporty	David	Arnaud	Julia
kind	Arnaud	Julia	David

3) a) Cette pièce est la plus passionnante.
   b) Je suis drôle, mais il est le plus drôle.
   c) Ces fleurs sont les plus jolies.

4) a) Tous les gâteaux sont bons mais les gâteaux au chocolat sont <u>les meilleurs</u>.
   b) Le foot est <u>pire que</u> le rugby.
   c) C'est en ville que la qualité de l'air est <u>la pire</u>.
   d) Mes notes ont été <u>meilleures que</u> l'année dernière.

5)

	bon	mauvais	bien	mal
Comparative	meilleur(e)	pire	mieux	pire
Superlative	le meilleur	le pire	le mieux	le pire

6) a) Pierre court <u>aussi vite que</u> Nadim. — as quickly as
   b) Tu joues au tennis <u>moins souvent que</u> Fred. — less often than
   c) Sam mange <u>plus tôt que</u> Laura. — earlier than

7) a) La situation est <u>pire</u> que ce matin.
      The situation is worse than this morning.
   b) Matthieu travaille <u>mieux</u> à l'école que Charles.
      Matthieu works better at school than Charles.

8) a) Je voyage moins souvent que toi.
   b) Henry joue mieux aux jeux vidéo que tous ses amis.
   c) Elle danse le mieux.
   d) Ma mère va le plus régulièrement au marché.

Section Fifteen —
Verbs and Tenses

Pages 88-89: Present Tense

1) a) Je <u>vais</u> en Suisse la semaine prochaine.
   b) J'<u>aime</u> les fruits et les légumes.
   c) C'<u>est</u> encore une journée de pluie.
   d) Tu <u>vois</u> ta tante le dimanche.
   e) Je <u>préfère</u> les films d'action.
   f) J'<u>ai</u> deux petits frères.
   g) Vous <u>faites</u> vos devoirs.
   h) Le mercredi, il <u>mange</u> seulement du fromage.
   i) Nous <u>détestons</u> le sport et la physique.
   j) Il y <u>a</u> des élèves très bavards dans ma classe.

2) a) mange
   b) donnons
   c) achetez
   d) finis
   e) choisissent
   f) partagez
   g) supportent
   h) suis
   i) cache
   j) attendez
   k) remplit
   l) vends

3) a) Il rest<u>e</u> à la maison parce qu'il regard<u>e</u> le match de foot à la télé.
   b) Nous habit<u>ons</u> dans un appartement au bord de la mer et vous pouv<u>ez</u> venir chez nous.
   c) Je man<u>ge</u> chez moi tous les jours à midi, mais mes amis man<u>gent</u> au café.
   d) Vous par<u>lez</u> à votre ami au téléphone, et elle vous par<u>le</u> de ses vacances.

4) a) Nous courons dans le parc.
   b) Tu joues au foot.
   c) Ils étudient chaque jour.
   d) Je prends des photos.
   e) Il écrit une histoire.
   f) Vous partez aujourd'hui.

5) a) suis
   b) es
   c) est
   d) sommes
   e) êtes
   f) sont

6) a) ai
   b) as
   c) a
   d) avons
   e) avez
   f) ont

7) a) fais
   b) vas
   c) veut
   d) devons
   e) faites
   f) fait
   g) allons
   h) voulez
   i) doivent
   j) sais

8) a) Il <u>boit</u> du thé.
   b) Ils <u>disent</u> toujours ça.
   c) Je <u>lis</u> un journal.
   d) Est-ce que vous <u>savez</u> danser ?
   e) Elles <u>prennent</u> beaucoup de photos.
   f) Vous <u>ouvrez</u> la porte.
   g) Est-ce que tu <u>veux</u> venir avec moi au cinéma ?
   h) Elle <u>doit</u> faire ses devoirs.
   i) Nous <u>pouvons</u> faire une promenade s'il fait beau.

Pages 90-91: Past Tenses

1) a) acheté
   b) dansé
   c) dormi
   d) caché
   e) mangé
   f) pris
   g) entendu
   h) venu
   i) fini
   j) joué
   k) vendu
   l) choisi

2) a) Ma belle-mère m'<u>a</u> donné de beaux cadeaux.
   b) Nous <u>avons</u> célébré l'anniversaire de mon père.
   c) Tu <u>as</u> porté un nouveau pantalon.
   d) Mes cousins <u>ont</u> mangé des frites.
   e) Vous <u>avez</u> trouvé un métier intéressant.

3) a) Tu <u>as mis</u> le repas sur la table.
   b) Il <u>a lu</u> le premier roman de son auteur préféré.
   c) Les parents <u>ont écrit</u> une lettre à leurs enfants.
   d) Vous <u>avez traduit</u> l'article en français.

4) a) Elle <u>est partie</u> après le concours.
   b) Il <u>est venu</u> me voir samedi après-midi.
   c) Mon petit frère <u>est tombé</u> malade à l'école.
   d) Nous <u>sommes entrées</u> dans la salle de classe.
   e) Ils <u>sont restés</u> ici pendant les vacances.
   f) Je <u>suis rentrée</u> au collège en septembre.

5) a) Tu <u>faisais</u> des gâteaux pour moi.
   b) Je <u>faisais</u> du vélo tous les matins.
   c) Qu'est-ce qu'elles <u>faisaient</u> hier soir ?
   d) Nous <u>faisions</u> beaucoup de devoirs tous les jours.

6) a) On <u>avait</u> toujours quelque chose à faire.
   b) J'<u>avais</u> trois leçons par semaine.
   c) Vous <u>aviez</u> mon adresse.
   d) Ils <u>avaient</u> des problèmes.

7) a) Tu <u>étais</u> très content de recevoir le prix.
   b) J'<u>étais</u> toujours en retard.
   c) Vous <u>étiez</u> très jeunes en 2006.
   d) Les films <u>étaient</u> assez amusants.

8) a) I was watching TV.
   b) We were waiting for the postman.
   c) He was singing in his bath.

9) a) Je jouais au foot.
   b) Tu allais au parc.
   c) Elle achetait le journal.

10) I have lived in England since 2007.

Pages 92-93: Talking about the Future & The Conditional

1) a) tu vas manger
   b) nous allons finir
   c) ils vont commencer
   d) vous allez prendre
   e) elles vont aller

2) a) Je vais lire les articles en ligne.
   b) Elles vont voyager en Europe.
   c) Tu vas organiser une grande fête.
   d) On va préparer le repas tôt.

3) a) j'aurai
   b) elle sera
   c) on dansera
   d) nous jouerons
   e) tu feras

4) a) Tu <u>oublieras</u> les lettres.
   b) On <u>regardera</u> un film très triste.
   c) Elle <u>ira</u> au supermarché demain.
   d) Vous <u>demanderez</u> la carte au restaurant.

5) a) Je voudrais une boisson, s'il vous plaît.
    b) Tu voudrais payer le vendeur.
    c) Elle voudrait rentrer à la maison.
    d) Il voudrait voir le concours.
    e) Est-ce que tu voudrais du thé ou du café ?
6) a) Je préférerais rester chez moi.
    b) Il aimerait manger le gâteau entier.
    c) Nous détesterions voir un match de foot.
    d) Je jouerais au basket si je n'avais pas mal à la jambe.
    e) Ils ont dit qu'ils voyageraient en train cet après-midi.
    f) Je le ferais si c'était moins difficile.
    g) Ils danseraient toute la nuit.
    h) J'irais au cinéma si j'avais le temps.
    i) Je serais heureux de vous voir.
    j) Si je n'étais pas malade, j'aurais du vin.
7) a) J'aimerais aller en France pour étudier.
    b) Vous achèteriez tous les sacs du magasin.
    c) Elle regarderait le film avec moi.
    d) Nous voudrions aider.

Pages 94-95: Reflexives, Negative Forms & Giving Orders

1) a) je me lave
    b) tu te laves
    c) il /elle se lave
    d) nous nous lavons
    e) vous vous lavez
    f) ils / elles se lavent
2) a) On se lave toujours à l'eau chaude.
    b) Tu te souviens de mon anniversaire ?
    c) L'appartement se trouve à l'autre côté du supermarché.
    d) S'il n'a pas de carte, il se perd toujours.
    e) Je ne me lève jamais avant sept heures du matin.
3) a) Ce matin, elle s'est levée à huit heures.
    b) Le couple s'est quitté après les vacances.
    c) Il s'est lavé trois fois après le match.
    d) Elles se sont préparées ensemble avant la fête.
    e) Nous nous sommes organisés pour le festival.
4) a) Je ne mange pas de fromage.
    b) Nous ne lavons pas nos vêtements.
    c) Ce n'est pas loin d'ici.
    d) Il ne lit pas de livres.
    e) Ce n'est pas la même chose.
    f) Je n'ai pas de billets.
5) a) Il n'a pas visité le château.
    b) Ils ne vont jamais au théâtre.
    c) Je ne suis jamais allée au collège.
    d) Il n'a rien compris.
    e) Personne n'a mangé de poisson.
6) a) Je n'ai pas encore regardé le nouveau film.
    b) Elle n'a qu'une heure pour terminer l'examen.
    c) Je ne vais plus manger de viande.
    d) L'hôtel n'est ni joli ni propre.

7) a) Finis tes devoirs !
    b) Francine et Agnès, venez avec nous !
    c) Mange tes légumes !
    d) Essaie / Essaye encore une fois !
    e) Sois plus positif !
    f) Soyez plus gentils !
    g) Allons au marché !
    h) Faisons un gâteau !

Pages 96-97: -ing Verbs, Impersonal Verbs & the Passive

1) a) donnant
    b) partant
    c) entendant
    d) achetant
    e) choisissant
    f) perdant
    g) faisant
    h) allant
    i) étant
2) a) J'ai joué du piano en parlant.
       I played the piano whilst talking.
    b) En entrant dans la cuisine, je vois mon père.
       As I enter the kitchen, I see my father.
    c) Nous avons expliqué la situation en marchant.
       We explained the situation whilst walking.
    d) Elle est entrée en riant.
       She entered whilst laughing.
    e) Il a crié en tombant.
       He shouted whilst falling.
3) a) Après avoir fait du pain, je l'ai mangé.
    b) Après être parti, il est revenu.
4) a) 5
    b) 1
    c) 4
    d) 3
    e) 2
5) a) 3
    b) 4
    c) 5
    d) 2
    e) 1
6) a) The animal is washed
    b) I am watched
    c) The letters are sent
    d) You are found
    e) The road was closed
7) a) Le repas est preparé par beaucoup de gens.
    b) La nourriture n'est pas mangée par Marc.
    c) Mes histoires sont aimées par les enfants.
    d) La chanson est écrite par mon frère.

107

Foundation Speaking Questions — Mark Scheme

It's very difficult to mark the speaking questions yourself because there isn't one 'right' answer for most questions. To make them easier to mark, record yourself and use a dictionary, or get someone who's really good at French to mark how well you did. Use the mark schemes below to help you, but bear in mind that they're only a rough guide. Ideally, you need a French teacher who knows the AQA mark schemes well to mark it properly.

Role-play (10 marks)

In the Role-play, you'll be marked on how accurately you respond to spoken language.
There are 2 marks available for each of the five tasks in the Role-play (10 marks in total).

Marks	Role-play task
2	You convey your message without ambiguity.
1	You partially convey your message with some ambiguity.
0	None of your message is conveyed.

Reading aloud (15 marks)

The Reading aloud task is divided into two parts. There are 5 marks available for reading the text aloud, and then 10 marks are available for answering the four compulsory questions.

Marks	Reading the text
5	Your pronunciation may contain minor errors and a few major errors.
4	Your pronunciation contains regular minor and some major errors.
3	Your pronunciation contains frequent minor and major errors.
2	Your pronunciation is rarely accurate.
1	Your pronunciation is very rarely accurate.
0	Does not meet the standard required for 1 mark.

Marks	Responding to the questions
9-10	You answer all questions clearly. At least two answers have an extended response and at least one other is developed well.
7-8	You answer at least three questions clearly. One answer has an extended response and at least one other is developed well.
5-6	You answer at least two questions clearly. One answer is developed well and at least one other is developed minimally.
3-4	You answer at least two questions understandably. One answer is developed minimally.
1-2	You answer at least one question understandably. The answer(s) may be a very limited response.
0	Does not meet the standard required for 1 mark.

Photo card (25 marks)

For the Photo card task, you're marked on three separate criteria. 5 marks are available for your response to the content of the photos on the card, whilst 20 marks are available for the unprepared conversation — 15 marks for 'communication' and 5 marks for 'grammar and vocabulary'.

Marks	Describing the photos
5	You convey quite a lot of information. Information may lack clarity from time to time.
4	You convey some information. Information lacks clarity from time to time.
3	You convey some information. Information lacks clarity from time to time and occasionally messages break down.
2	You convey little information. Messages regularly break down.
1	You convey very little information. Messages regularly break down or the language produced is barely understandable.
0	Does not meet the standard required for 1 mark.

Marks	Unprepared conversation — communication
13-15	You convey quite a lot of information and regularly develop your responses well. Information may lack clarity from time to time.
10-12	You convey some information. You develop some responses well and regularly develop responses minimally. Information lacks clarity from time to time.
7-9	You convey some information and there is regular minimal development of your responses. Information lacks clarity from time to time and occasionally messages break down.
4-6	You convey little information and give limited responses with occasional minimal development. Messages regularly break down.
1-3	You convey very little information with limited responses. Messages regularly break down or hardly anything is said.
0	Does not meet the standard required for 1 mark.

Marks	Unprepared conversation — grammar and vocabulary
5	You use a good variety of vocabulary and structures, but with some repetition. You make frequent minor errors. Some major errors may occur even in basic language.
4	You use some variety of vocabulary and structures, but with regular repetition. You make frequent minor errors and some major errors in most responses to questions.
3	You use a limited variety of vocabulary and structures with regular repetition. You make very frequent minor and frequent major errors in most responses to questions.
2	You use a very limited variety of vocabulary and structures with regular repetition. You make very frequent minor and major errors in nearly all responses to questions.
1	You use hardly any variety of vocabulary and structures. You make minor and major errors in all responses to questions.
0	Does not meet the standard required for 1 mark.

Find the CGP RevisionHub at cgpbooks.co.uk/cafe

Answers

Higher Speaking Questions — Mark Scheme

Role-play (10 marks)

In the Role-play, you'll be marked on how accurately you respond to spoken language. There are 2 marks available for each of the five tasks in the Role-play (10 marks in total). If you are required to give two responses or details in one task, failure to convey an unambiguous message in reply to one of them means that the message is partially conveyed and one mark is awarded.

Marks	Role-play task
2	You convey your message without ambiguity.
1	You partially convey your message with some ambiguity.
0	None of your message is conveyed.

Reading aloud (15 marks)

The Reading aloud task is divided into two parts. There are 5 marks available for reading the text aloud, and then 10 marks are available for answering the four compulsory questions.

Marks	Reading the text
5	Your pronunciation is always or nearly always accurate but you may make an occasional minor error.
4	Your pronunciation contains a few minor errors.
3	Your pronunciation contains some minor errors and very occasional major errors.
2	Your pronunciation contains minor errors and a few major errors.
1	Your pronunciation contains regular minor and some major errors.
0	Does not meet the standard required for 1 mark.

Marks	Responding to the questions
9-10	You answer all questions clearly. At least two answers have an extended response and at least one other is developed well.
7-8	You answer at least three questions clearly. One answer has an extended response and at least one other is developed well.
5-6	You answer at least two questions clearly. One answer is developed well and at least one other is developed minimally.
3-4	You answer at least two questions understandably. One answer is developed minimally.
1-2	You answer at least one question understandably. The answer(s) may be a very limited response.
0	Does not meet the standard required for 1 mark.

Photo card (25 marks)

For the Photo card task, you're marked on three separate criteria. 5 marks are available for your response to the content of the photos on the card, whilst 20 marks are available for the unprepared conversation — 15 marks for 'communication' and 5 marks for 'grammar and vocabulary'.

Marks	Describing the photos
5	You convey a lot of information. Information is always conveyed clearly.
4	You convey a lot of information. Information is nearly always conveyed clearly.
3	You convey quite a lot of information. Information is nearly always conveyed clearly.
2	You convey quite a lot of information. Information may lack clarity from time to time.
1	You convey some information. Information may lack clarity from time to time.
0	Does not meet the standard required for 1 mark.

Marks	Unprepared conversation — communication
13-15	You convey a lot of information with consistent good development and regular extended responses. Information is always or nearly always conveyed clearly.
10-12	You convey a lot of information with consistent good development and some extended responses. Information is conveyed clearly, with occasional lapses.
7-9	You convey quite a lot of information with consistent good development and occasional extended responses. Information is generally conveyed clearly.
4-6	You convey quite a lot of information with regular good development of responses. Information may lack clarity from time to time.
1-3	You convey some information with good development and regular minimal development of responses. Information may lack clarity from time to time.
0	Does not meet the standard required for 1 mark.

Marks	Unprepared conversation — grammar and vocabulary
5	You use a wide variety of vocabulary and structures. You make a few minor errors but few or no major errors when you attempt more complex language.
4	You use a very good variety of vocabulary and structures. You make some minor errors and some major errors when you attempt more complex language.
3	You use a good variety of vocabulary and structures with occasional repetition. You make quite a lot of minor errors and occasional major errors, not only in attempts at more complex language.
2	You use a good variety of vocabulary and structures with some repetition. You make frequent minor errors and some major errors, even with basic language.
1	You use some variety of vocabulary and structures but with regular repetition. You make frequent minor errors and some major errors in most responses to questions.
0	Does not meet the standard required for 1 mark.

Answers

Foundation Writing Questions — Mark Scheme

As with the speaking questions, it's difficult to mark the writing questions yourself because there are no 'right' answers. You ideally need a French teacher who knows the AQA mark schemes to mark your answers properly. Each of the writing tasks has a different mark scheme.

Photo Question (10 marks)

For this question, you're required to write five sentences to describe a photo. There are 2 marks available for each of the five sentences (10 marks in total).

Marks	Communication
2	You convey a relevant message clearly.
1	You convey a relevant message with some ambiguity which causes a delay in communication.
0	Your message is irrelevant or cannot be understood.

10-mark Writing Question

For this question, there are five compulsory bullet points. There are 5 marks available for 'Communication' and 5 marks for 'Grammar and vocabulary'.

Marks	Communication
5	You cover all five bullet points and communicate clearly.
4	You cover at least four bullet points. Your communication is mostly clear with occasional lapses in clarity.
3	You cover at least three bullet points. Your communication is generally clear with several lapses in clarity.
2	You cover at least two bullet points. Your communication is sometimes clear with regular lapses in clarity.
1	You cover at least one bullet point. Your communication is often not clear with many lapses in clarity.
0	Does not meet the standard required for 1 mark.

Marks	Grammar and vocabulary
5	You use a variety of vocabulary and grammatical structures with some minor errors.
4	You use some variety of vocabulary and grammatical structures. You make frequent minor errors with an occasional major error.
3	You attempt to use a variety of vocabulary and grammatical structures. You make frequent minor errors with some major errors.
2	You use limited or repetitive vocabulary and grammatical structures. You make frequent minor errors and a number of major errors.
1	You show little awareness of appropriate vocabulary and grammatical structures. You make errors in the vast majority of sentences.
0	Does not meet the standard required for 1 mark.

15-mark Writing Question

For this question, there are three compulsory bullet points that you must cover — you don't need to cover the bullet points equally. There are 10 marks available for 'Communication' and 5 marks for 'Grammar and vocabulary'.

Marks	Communication
9-10	You cover all three bullet points and communicate clearly. Your ideas are regularly developed and you convey a lot of relevant information.
7-8	You cover all three bullet points and your communication is mostly clear with occasional lapses in clarity. Your ideas are often developed and you convey quite a lot of relevant information.
5-6	You cover at least two bullet points and your communication is generally clear with some lapses in clarity. A few of your ideas may be developed and some relevant information is conveyed.
3-4	You cover at least one bullet point and your communication is sometimes clear with regular lapses in clarity. You convey little relevant information.
1-2	You cover at least one bullet point. Your communication is often not clear and there are very many lapses in clarity. You convey very little relevant information.
0	Does not meet the standard required for 1 mark.

Marks	Grammar and vocabulary
5	You use a good variety of vocabulary with regular attempts at complex language and structures. You make successful references to all three time frames. Errors are mainly minor but you may make some major errors, particularly in complex structures and sentences.
4	You use a variety of vocabulary with some attempts at complex language and structures. You make mainly successful references to at least two different time frames. You make mainly minor errors and some major errors.
3	You use a variety of vocabulary and occasionally attempt complex language and structures. You make references to at least two time frames, although these may not always be successful. You make some major errors and regular minor errors but overall the response is more accurate than inaccurate.
2	You use a limited variety of vocabulary and use mainly simple language with some attempts at longer sentences using appropriate linking words. You may not reference different time frames successfully. You make frequent major and minor errors and your response is generally inaccurate.
1	You use a narrow and/or repetitive range of vocabulary. You use simple language and short sentences that may not be properly constructed. You make no successful references to different time frames. You make frequent major and minor errors and overall your response is highly inaccurate.
0	Does not meet the standard required for 1 mark.

Higher Writing Questions — Mark Scheme

15-mark Writing Question

For this question, there are three compulsory bullet points that you must cover — you don't need to cover the bullet points equally. There are 10 marks available for 'Communication' and 5 marks for 'Grammar and vocabulary'.

Marks	Communication
9-10	You cover all three bullet points and communicate clearly. Your ideas are developed and you convey a lot of information.
7-8	You cover all three bullet points and mostly communicate clearly. Your ideas are often developed and you convey quite a lot of information.
5-6	You cover at least two bullet points and generally communicate clearly. You develop a few ideas and convey some information.
3-4	You cover at least one bullet point and sometimes communicate clearly. You convey little information.
1-2	You cover at least one bullet point. Your communication is often unclear and you convey very little information.
0	Does not meet the standard required for 1 mark.

Marks	Grammar and vocabulary
5	You use a good variety of vocabulary with complex language and structures. You use all three time frames and any errors are mainly minor.
4	You use a variety of vocabulary and attempt to use complex language and structures. You use at least two time frames and errors are mainly minor.
3	You use some variety of vocabulary and occasionally attempt complex language and structures. You try to use at least two time frames. There are regular minor errors and may be some major errors.
2	You use a limited variety of vocabulary and use mainly simple language. You might fail to use different time frames and make regular errors.
1	Your vocabulary is narrow and/or repetitive. You use simple language and structures. You fail to use different time frames and make frequent errors.
0	Does not meet the standard required for 1 mark.

25-mark Writing Question

For this question, there are two compulsory bullet points that you must cover — you don't need to cover the bullet points equally. There are 15 marks available for 'Communication', 5 marks for 'Range of language' and 5 marks for 'Accuracy of language'.

Marks	Communication
13-15	You convey a lot of information with very few or no lapses in clarity. Your ideas are regularly developed.
10-12	You convey quite a lot of information, and communication is mostly clear with occasional lapses in clarity. Your ideas are often developed.
7-9	You convey an adequate amount of information, and communication is usually clear with some lapses in clarity. A few of your ideas may be developed.
4-6	You convey some information, but communication is sometimes unclear with regular lapses in clarity. There is only a little development of your ideas.
1-3	You convey a limited amount of information, and communication is unclear with frequent lapses in clarity. There is very limited development of ideas.
0	Does not meet the standard required for 1 mark.

Marks	Range of language
5	You use a very good variety of appropriate vocabulary and grammatical structures with regular successful attempts at complex language.
4	You use a good variety of appropriate vocabulary and grammatical structures with regular, generally successful attempts at complex language.
3	You use some variety of appropriate vocabulary and grammatical structures with occasional, sometimes successful attempts at complex language.
2	You use a limited variety of vocabulary and grammatical structures. You often use short and simple structures but also regularly use longer sentences.
1	You use a very limited variety of appropriate vocabulary. You mainly use short and simple structures.
0	Does not meet the standard required for 1 mark.

Marks	Accuracy of language
5	Your response is usually accurate, with occasional errors in attempts at more complex structures. Your verb and tense formations are secure.
4	Your response is generally accurate, with several errors in attempts at more complex structures. Your verb and tense formations are generally correct.
3	Your response is reasonably accurate, with errors in both simple and complex structures. Your verb and tense formations are sometimes correct.
2	Your response is more inaccurate than accurate. There are frequent errors. Your verb and tense formations are often incorrect.
1	Your response is mostly inaccurate and there are errors in all sentences. Your verb and tense formations are nearly always incorrect.
0	Does not meet the standard required for 1 mark.

Answers

Listening Transcripts

You can find printable versions of the Listening and Speaking transcripts on the CGP RevisionHub — go to cgpbooks.co.uk/cafe.

Section One — General Stuff

Listening Track 1 — p.2

1a) **M1:** Mon week-end était génial ! J'ai fait du shopping et j'ai acheté trois sacs.
1b) **M1:** Puis, je suis allé à la poste pour envoyer huit lettres aux membres de ma famille qui vivent à l'étranger.
1c) **M1:** Finalement, j'ai acheté un billet de train pour rentrer chez moi. Tout ça m'a coûté cent cinquante-six euros.
1d) **M1:** J'ai passé samedi soir avec cinq de mes copains, parce que c'était le seizième anniversaire de mon meilleur ami.
1e) **M1:** Il a de la chance — il a reçu une dizaine de cadeaux.

Listening Track 2 — p.3

4a) **F1:** Il est né | le dix avril.
4b) **M1:** J'ai acheté | quatorze melons.
4c) **M1:** Il est | dix-huit heures.
4d) **F1:** Je trouve l'été | splendide.

Listening Track 3 — p.4

2a) **F2:** Bienvenue au | château royal.
2b) **M2:** Félicitations pour | ton succès à l'examen.
2c) **F2:** Attention | à la route.
2d) **M2:** Voici la porte | d'entrée.

Listening Track 4 — p.6

2a) **M1:** Salut Léa ! Comment ça va ?
   F2: Salut Rachid ! Ça va très bien, merci. Je viens d'assister à un concert de Sabrina, ma chanteuse préférée. Est-ce que tu aimes ses chansons ?
2b) **M1:** Elle ne m'intéresse pas. Je crois qu'elle n'écrit pas ses propres chansons.
2c) **F2:** Tu as tort ! À mon avis, elle est étonnante, et ses spectacles sont toujours extraordinaires.
2d) **M1:** L'objectif principal de toutes les célébrités, c'est de gagner de l'argent.

Section Two — Identity and Relationships with Others

Listening Track 5 — p.9

4a) **F1:** Je suis née dans | un pays européen.
4b) **F1:** J'ai une vie de famille | très heureuse.
4c) **F1:** Ma maman est gentille. | Elle aide toujours les autres.
4d) **F1:** Mes parents | me manquent beaucoup.

Listening Track 6 — p.11

4a) **F1:** Bonjour et bienvenue à « L'heure des questions ». Aujourd'hui, nous allons parler du mariage. Sylvie, quelle est ton opinion sur le mariage ?
   F2: Je suis contre l'idée du mariage. Je préférerais rester célibataire parce que je voudrais être indépendante.
4b) **F1:** Et toi, Richard, qu'est-ce que tu penses du mariage ?
   M2: Je voudrais me marier et avoir des enfants. Je sors avec ma copine depuis trois ans, mais elle n'est pas prête à se marier.

Section Three — Healthy Living and Lifestyle

Listening Track 7 — p.12

1a) **M2:** Bien manger, c'est très important. Je mange toujours cinq fruits ou légumes par jour.
1b) **F1:** Mon médecin m'a recommandé la danse comme exercice. Pour rester en bonne santé, je dois danser trois fois par semaine.
1c) **F2:** Pour être en bonne santé, il ne faut se coucher ni trop tôt ni trop tard. Il faut absolument bien dormir.

Listening Track 8 — p.15

4a) **F1:** Mon copain a mal | à la jambe.
4b) **M1:** Il est | très fatigué.
4c) **F1:** Demain il va aller | à l'hôpital.
4d) **M1:** Il veut changer | de médicaments.

Section Four — Education

Listening Track 9 — p.16

2a) **M2:** Bonjour Inès ! Est-ce que tu aimes les langues ?
   F1: Pour moi, les langues ne sont pas aussi utiles que les sciences. Je préfère la physique mais je trouve que toutes les sciences sont importantes. En plus, les langues sont difficiles pour moi.
2b) **F1:** Et toi, Yasmina ?
   F2: Je ne suis pas de ton avis. Pour moi, la matière de l'avenir, c'est l'informatique — il faut comprendre la technologie pour vivre mieux. J'adore passer mon temps devant l'ordinateur.
2c) **F2:** Tu ne partages pas cet avis, Mehdi ?
   M2: Je crois que les jeunes comptent trop sur les ordinateurs et passent trop de temps devant des écrans. Je trouve aussi qu'on doit être fort en maths, en sciences, en français et en anglais. Il ne faut pas toujours utiliser un ordinateur.

Listening Track 10 — p.18

1a) **M1:** Pour moi, le plus grand problème à l'école, c'est que les profs nous donnent trop de devoirs. Ils nous disent qu'il faut les faire pour bien se préparer pour les examens, mais quatre heures le soir, c'est trop ! Je n'aime pas les devoirs, et je n'aime pas les examens.
1b) **F2:** Je crois que le comportement des élèves est un grand défi — il y en a certains qui ne s'intéressent pas aux cours, qui discutent quand le prof parle et qui harcèlent les autres élèves dans la cour. Par contre, je trouve que les règles scolaires sont souvent trop strictes.

Section Five — Future Study and Work

Listening Track 11 — p.20

2a) **M1:** Salut Marie ! Quel est ton travail ?
   F1: Je suis directrice d'école.
2b) **F1:** Et toi, Enzo ?
   M1: Moi, je suis aidant.
2c) **M1:** Est-ce que tu aimes ton métier, Dorian ?
   M2: Je n'aime pas être serveur car il faut toujours travailler le week-end.
2d) **M2:** Et toi, Fathia ?
   F2: J'aime aider le public. C'est pourquoi je suis policière.

Theme 1 — Mixed Practice

Listening Track 12 — p.24

5a) **M1:** Dans mon collège, les profs sont géniaux — ils m'aident beaucoup.

5b) **F1:** J'ai toujours eu beaucoup de problèmes au lycée et je m'inquiète toujours, surtout pendant les examens.

5c) **F2:** J'adore la grande bibliothèque de mon collège. Cependant, les toilettes sont très sales.

5d) **M2:** Les autres élèves de mon collège ne sont pas méchants et on s'entend bien.

Listening Track 13 — p.25

1a) **F1:** Est-ce que vous préférez un travail actif ? Est-ce que vous voulez rencontrer des membres du public ? La poste cherche de nouveaux facteurs dans votre ville. Vous ne devez pas avoir peur des chiens. Savoir faire du vélo est un avantage.

1b) **M1:** Nous cherchons des jeunes pour travailler dans notre hôtel l'été prochain. Il faut pouvoir travailler en équipe, mais il n'y a pas besoin de savoir conduire. C'est votre personnalité et vos compétences qui sont importantes.

1c) **F2:** Est-ce que vous aimez les enfants ? Et travailler avec le public ? Est-ce que vous êtes toujours professionnel ? Si votre réponse est oui, ce boulot est parfait pour vous. Nous cherchons des jeunes qui ont déjà passé le bac pour travailler dans notre club de vacances six jours par semaine. C'est un travail qui n'est pas toujours facile mais qui vous donnera beaucoup d'expérience pour votre carrière à l'avenir.

Listening Track 14 — p.26

3a) **M1:** Mon frère | est petit.

3b) **F1:** Elle avait | les cheveux noirs | et les yeux marron.

3c) **M1:** Je ressemble beaucoup à | ma mère.

3d) **F1:** Je respecte toujours | mon oncle | italien.

Listening Track 15 — p.27

5a) **F2:** Hier, j'ai essayé de voir le médecin, mais il n'y avait pas de rendez-vous disponible. Ce manque de rendez-vous est un problème grave.

5b) **M1:** Selon moi, les médecins sont vraiment extraordinaires.

5c) **F1:** La plupart des employés des hôpitaux sont formidables. Cependant, un expert m'a donné de très mauvais conseils.

5d) **M2:** Beaucoup de gens souffrent à cause des longues heures d'attente pour obtenir des soins médicaux.

Listening Track 16 — p.27

6a) **M2:** Qu'est-ce que tu penses des cigarettes, Myriam ?
F2: Je ne fume pas. Je pense que les cigarettes sont dégoûtantes. Je déteste quand les autres fument parce que ça peut créer des problèmes de santé.

6b) **M2:** Et toi, Jules, quel est ton avis ?
M1: Moi, je fume et j'aime fumer. Je sais que ce n'est pas sain, mais fumer m'aide à me relaxer. Ma copine dit que je dois essayer de fumer moins souvent.

6c) **M2:** Fatima, qu'est-ce que tu en penses ?
F1: Moi, j'ai fumé pendant longtemps, mais j'ai arrêté l'année dernière. Les conseils des experts m'ont aidée à comprendre que fumer, c'est vraiment mauvais pour la santé.

Listening Track 17 — p.28

1a) **M2:** Il travaille pour | un établissement indépendant.

1b) **F2:** La concurrence est énorme | dans ce secteur.

1c) **M2:** Je veux créer | de nouvelles lois.

1d) **F2:** Je suis prête pour | la prochaine étape.

Listening Track 18 — p.31

9a) **F1:** Zoé, j'ai récemment réfléchi à ma carrière. Je dois admettre que je voudrais changer de métier.

9b) **F2:** Morgane, est-ce que tu as pensé à prendre une année sabbatique ? J'ai pris une année sabbatique et c'était une bonne décision parce que maintenant je sais ce que je veux faire.

9c) **F1:** C'est une possibilité, mais je ne veux pas voyager. Je préférerais apprendre de nouvelles compétences.

9d) **F2:** Pourquoi ne pas étudier ? Tu t'intéresses à la recherche depuis longtemps.

Section Six — Free-time Activities

Listening Track 19 — p.33

3a) **M1:** Bienvenue, Lucie. Est-ce que tu as regardé la nouvelle série à la télé hier soir ?
F1: Salut Sofiane. Oui, c'était formidable à mon avis. J'ai surtout aimé les scènes avec les effets spéciaux.

3b) **M1:** Et Luis, qu'est-ce que tu en penses ?
M2: Selon moi, les effets spéciaux étaient nuls, et généralement je n'aime pas les séries de ce genre. Je pense qu'il y avait aussi trop de pubs.

Listening Track 20 — p.35

3a) **M2:** Salut Léa ! Récemment, je suis allé dans un nouveau restaurant. Mais, j'ai eu une mauvaise expérience. J'ai attendu longtemps pour obtenir une table et le serveur était paresseux.

3b) **M2:** Mais, le pire, c'était le bruit, qui était difficile à supporter.

3c) **F1:** Salut Rachid ! Heureusement, ça semblait plus tranquille quand j'y suis allée, mais je n'y retournerai jamais. Pour moi, le principal problème, c'était la nourriture. Le repas était froid, et je crois que, pour deux personnes, c'était trop cher.

Section Seven — Customs, Festivals and Celebrations

Listening Track 21 — p.36

2a) **F1:** Salut Zoé, qu'est-ce que tu as fait pour célébrer la Saint-Valentin ?
F2: Salut ! Cette année, ma copine et moi sommes allées à un festival de musique au Québec. C'était une expérience géniale.

2b) **F1:** Et alors, tu as reçu un cadeau ?
F2: Oui, ma copine m'a donné des fleurs et un petit cadeau. Je ne l'ai pas ouvert jusqu'à notre voyage le lendemain.

2c) **F1:** Qu'est-ce que tu penses de la Saint-Valentin ?
F2: À mon avis, c'est un jour très spécial. C'est un jour idéal pour montrer son amour à quelqu'un.

Section Eight — Celebrity Culture

Listening Track 22 — p.38

2a) **F2:** Je ne veux pas | être célèbre.

2b) **M2:** L'auteur vend | des millions | de livres.

2c) **F2:** Je m'inspire de | plusieurs acteurs | formidables.

2d) **M2:** Les célébrités créent | leurs propres marques.

Theme 2 — Mixed Practice

Listening Track 23 — p.42

6a) **F1:** Pour les personnes célèbres, rencontrer de vrais amis est difficile parce que leurs vies sont très publiques.

6b) **F2:** Je pense que les stars ont trop d'influence sur les jeunes. Mais parfois, elles peuvent utiliser leur succès pour aider les autres.

6c) **M1:** À mon avis, les médias partagent souvent de fausses informations sur les célébrités. Ça peut causer une crise d'identité.

6d) **M2:** Les célébrités gagnent beaucoup d'argent. Alors, elles peuvent voyager et acheter de belles maisons.

Listening Track 24 — p.43

1a) **M1:** Mon frère | est très sportif.
1b) **F1:** Je n'aime pas | regarder la télé.
1c) **M1:** Je vais réserver | une table | pour deux.
1d) **F1:** On joue | dans une petite équipe | locale.

Listening Track 25 — p.44

4a) **M2:** L'Aïd est une grande fête musulmane. Pour la célébrer, on partage un repas spécial et tout le monde porte de beaux vêtements.
4b) **M2:** Dans ma famille, les adultes donnent de petits cadeaux aux enfants. On écoute de la musique traditionnelle et on danse beaucoup. C'est vraiment une fête super.

Listening Track 26 — p.45

5a) **M2:** Mon copain va | au temple chaque semaine.
5b) **F2:** J'adore célébrer | la Saint-Valentin.
5c) **M2:** J'ai toujours eu | une foi profonde.
5d) **F2:** N'oubliez pas | d'apporter | du jus de fruits.

Listening Track 27 — p.46

8a) **F1:** Sabrina, est-ce que vous pensez que vous allez gagner un prix ce soir ?
   F2: Je ne sais pas ! Mon amie Sylvie était excellente dans son dernier film.
8b) **F1:** Et Patrick, comment ça va avec Sabrina ?
   M2: Nous sommes très contents, merci. Le mois dernier, nous avons acheté une maison sur une île de la Méditerranée.
8c) **F1:** Super ! Et alors, Sabrina, on sait que vous êtes aussi chanteuse. Est-ce que vous avez des projets dans le proche avenir ?
   F2: Oui, mon groupe et moi allons écrire de nouvelles chansons bientôt, puis nous espérons faire des concerts partout dans le monde.

Listening Track 28 — p.49

6a) **F1:** Je suis Camille. Hier, j'ai vu une émission qui explique le développement des médicaments modernes.
6b) **F1:** Il y avait quelques scènes étonnantes.
6c) **M1:** Je suis Alex. Moi, je regarderai une nouvelle série cette semaine — elle raconte l'histoire d'une guerre sur une autre planète en deux mille cent cinquante.
6d) **M1:** Je la trouve passionnante et j'apprécie les effets spéciaux.

Section Nine — Travel and Tourism

Listening Track 29 — p.50

2a) **M1:** Où passes-tu tes vacances, Yasmina ?
   F2: Chaque été, je pars avec mes copains et on fait une promenade à la montagne. Nous prenons une carte, notre nourriture et nos vêtements.
2b) **F2:** Et toi, Mehdi ?
   M1: Le camping, ce n'est pas pour moi. Je préfère passer du temps au bord de la mer dans un grand hôtel avec un bon restaurant. J'aime surtout la cuisine locale en Méditerranée. Heureusement, ce sont mes parents qui paient.
2c) **M1:** Et toi, Chloé ?
   F1: L'année dernière, nous avons passé quelques jours dans un appartement en Belgique. Ce n'était pas cher, mais les chambres étaient sales et les toilettes ne marchaient pas. Cette année, je pense que nous allons rester chez nous !

Listening Track 30 — p.52

2a) **M1:** J'achète | une pomme.
2b) **F1:** La grotte ferme | à seize heures.
2c) **M1:** Il y a beaucoup | de touristes.
2d) **F1:** L'entrée du château | n'est pas ici.

Section Ten — Media and Technology

Listening Track 31 — p.54

1a) **F2:** Je m'appelle Fatima. Moi, j'aime bien la technologie, parce qu'on peut découvrir de nouvelles choses en ligne. J'utilise une application pour apprendre l'espagnol.
1b) **M2:** Je suis Mohamed. J'aime Internet, mais je trouve que les jeunes passent trop de temps devant un écran. En plus, on ne peut pas éviter l'influence de la publicité en ligne.

Listening Track 32 — p.57

4a) **M1:** Bonjour Clara. Est-ce que tu aimes les réseaux sociaux ?
   F1: J'adore les réseaux sociaux parce que je peux chatter avec ma meilleure amie. Elle habite à l'étranger, mais je parle avec elle tous les jours.
4b) **F1:** Et toi, Jules ?
   M1: Moi, j'utilise les réseaux sociaux pour partager des photos et des vidéos. Je pense que c'est génial de pouvoir montrer ma vie aux autres. C'est pourquoi j'adore suivre les influenceurs.
4c) **M1:** Tu utilises les réseaux sociaux, Chloé ?
   F2: Oui, j'utilise les réseaux sociaux. Cependant, je sais qu'Internet peut être dangereux. Je pense qu'on partage trop d'informations en ligne. Au collège, on a reçu des conseils pour se protéger des risques en ligne.

Section Eleven — Where People Live

Listening Track 33 — p.58

1a) **M1:** Il n'y a pas beaucoup d'espaces publics dans cette ville. C'est nul.
1b) **F1:** La nouvelle gare est parfaite et les trains arrivent toujours à l'heure.
1c) **F2:** On a la chance d'avoir plusieurs magasins de vêtements à la mode au centre-ville. Par contre, les rues y sont trop étroites.
1d) **M2:** Selon moi, c'est ennuyeux d'habiter ici parce qu'il n'y a rien à faire. Le conseil régional doit créer plus d'endroits pour les jeunes.

Listening Track 34 — p.60

2a) **M1:** Bonjour, je suis Ahmed et je suis venu pour aller au supermarché.
2b) **M1:** Les autres supermarchés sont trop loin de chez moi, alors je préfère faire mes courses ici.
2c) **F1:** Je m'appelle Nadia et j'ai passé la journée dans les magasins de vêtements. Cependant, je n'ai rien acheté parce que tout était trop cher.
2d) **F1:** Maintenant je cherche la sortie pour rentrer chez moi.
2e) **M2:** Bonjour, je suis Dorian. Je pense que c'est efficace de faire du shopping dans ce centre commercial car on trouve tout ici. C'est aussi une bonne façon de soutenir l'économie locale, ce qui est important.

Section Twelve — Environmental and Social Issues

Listening Track 35 — p.62

1a) **F1:** Le recyclage est très important parce qu'il nous aide à utiliser moins de ressources naturelles.
1b) **F1:** Tout le monde peut aider à améliorer la situation. Chaque personne doit recycler ses propres déchets. Il faut aussi essayer d'acheter moins de produits en plastique.
1c) **F1:** On peut recycler les boîtes et les sacs en plastique.

Listening Track 36 — p.65

4a) **M1:** Six personnes sont à l'hôpital après une manifestation à Lyon hier soir. La police a travaillé pendant trois heures pour mettre fin à la violence.

4b) **M1:** La semaine dernière à Paris, quelques associations ont organisé une journée d'événements sportifs. Le but était de soutenir les familles vivant dans la pauvreté.

4c) **M1:** Un porte-parole du Président a déclaré que le sud de la France est en état de crise, parce qu'en 24 heures, il est tombé un mois de pluie.

Theme 3 — Mixed Practice

Listening Track 37 — p.68

5a) **F1:** Moi, je déteste mes voisins et je trouve que ma maison est trop petite.

5b) **M1:** Il n'y a rien à faire et il pleut beaucoup.

Listening Track 38 — p.71

3a) **F2:** Elle est arrivée | au port hier soir.
3b) **M2:** Je n'aime pas | prendre l'avion.
3c) **F2:** Notre retour était | vraiment stressant.
3d) **M2:** Ils ne veulent pas | rentrer chez eux.

Listening Track 39 — p.72

1a) **F2:** Bonjour. Je cherche des informations. Comment peut-on se rendre au château ?

1b) **M2:** La gare n'est pas loin. On peut aussi y aller en voiture. Malheureusement, il n'y a pas de bus.

1c) **F2:** Est-ce que vous avez d'autres informations sur la visite ?
M2: Oui. Le billet coûte cinq euros. Vous pouvez profiter d'une belle vue sur la campagne autour du château, mais malheureusement vous ne pouvez pas prendre de photos dans le bâtiment.

Listening Track 40 — p.73

3a) **F1:** Si vous prenez le train aujourd'hui, il faut savoir qu'il y a beaucoup de retards. Achetez votre billet avant d'arriver à la gare pour éviter les problèmes. Ne prenez pas le risque de manquer le train.

3b) **M1:** On parle beaucoup des risques des communautés en ligne pour les jeunes. Beaucoup d'adolescents ont des comptes sur les réseaux sociaux, mais trop de jeunes souffrent parce que d'autres les harcèlent sur Internet.

3c) **F2:** Selon une nouvelle étude, beaucoup d'espèces disparaissent à une vitesse inquiétante. Les forêts où habitent ces animaux brûlent, ce qui mène à leur mort. La situation devient pire.

Listening Track 41 — p.74

5a) **M2:** Voici la météo mondiale de cette semaine. Lundi, il fera très froid en Tunisie.

5b) **M2:** Mardi, il y aura de la neige partout en Europe, donc évitez de conduire si possible.

5c) **M2:** À Londres, il va pleuvoir mercredi pendant la journée, mais la pluie arrêtera ce soir.

5d) **M2:** Enfin, il y aura des vents forts en Corse jeudi.

Listening Track 42 — p.75

7a) **F1:** En 1989, la police a découvert une jeune fille dans un champ loin d'une ville. Elle y vivait depuis des années, toute seule.

7b) **F1:** Chaque nuit, elle dormait dans une vieille tour parce qu'il faisait trop froid dans la forêt. La tour avait des murs énormes, et la jeune fille s'y sentait en sécurité.

7c) **F1:** Elle mangeait des fruits de la forêt, mais elle les lavait toujours avant de les manger, parce qu'il est très dangereux de tomber malade loin d'un hôpital.

7d) **F1:** Elle a beaucoup appris en vivant dans la nature et elle s'est inspirée de cette expérience quand elle a grandi. C'est pourquoi elle a choisi de s'occuper des oiseaux.

Speaking Transcripts

You can find printable versions of the Listening and Speaking transcripts on the CGP RevisionHub — go to cgpbooks.co.uk/cafe.

Section Three — Healthy Living and Lifestyle

Speaking Track 1 — Photo card — p.12

Intro: Parle-moi des photos.
2a) Est-ce que tu aimes faire de l'exercice ? Pourquoi ? / pourquoi pas ?
2b) Qu'est-ce que tu penses du sport dans ton école ?
2c) Quelle sorte de nourriture aimes-tu ? Pourquoi ?
2d) Quel est ton avis sur le fast-food ?

Section Four — Education

Speaking Track 2 — Reading aloud — p.16

Intro: Lis-moi le texte.
1a) Parle-moi de ta journée à l'école.
1b) Qu'est-ce que tu as fait pendant la récré hier ?
1c) Que penses-tu des devoirs ?
1d) Quelle est ta matière préférée ? Pourquoi ?

Section Five — Future Study and Work

Speaking Track 3 — Role-play — p.21

Intro: Tu parles avec ton amie marocaine. Moi, je suis ton amie.
1) Décris ton emploi idéal.
2) Est-ce que tu voudrais aller à l'université ? Pourquoi ?
3) The student will now ask the teacher a question. The teacher should answer.
4) Qu'est-ce que tu voudrais faire pendant une année sabbatique ?
5) Parle-moi d'une des matières que tu étudies. Pourquoi as-tu choisi cette matière ?

Theme 1 — Mixed Practice

Speaking Track 4 — Reading aloud — p.23

Intro: Lis-moi le texte.
3a) Qui est ton professeur préféré ?
3b) Quelle est ta matière préférée ? Pourquoi ?
3c) Est-ce que tu veux aller à l'université ?
3d) Qu'est-ce que tu penses des concours pour l'université ?

Speaking Track 5 — Photo card — p.29

Intro: Parle-moi des photos.
3a) Qu'est-ce que tu veux faire après l'école ?
3b) Est-ce que tu aimerais travailler dans un bureau ? Pourquoi ?
3c) Que font tes parents comme travail ?
3d) Quelle est la chose la plus importante dans un travail ?

Speaking Track 6 — Reading aloud — p.30

Intro: Lis-moi le texte.
5a) Quel est ton plat préféré ?
5b) Comment est-ce que tu gardes la forme ?
5c) Est-ce que tu voudrais devenir médecin ? Pourquoi / pourquoi pas ?
5d) Quels sont les dangers des cigarettes ?

Speaking Track 7 — Role-play — p.31

Intro: Tu parles avec ton ami français. Moi, je suis ton ami.
1) Décris la personnalité d'un de tes amis.
2) Décris-moi un des membres de ta famille.
3) The student will now ask the teacher a question. The teacher should answer.
4) Est-ce que tu voudrais avoir des enfants plus tard ? Pourquoi ? / pourquoi pas ?
5) Qu'est-ce que tu as fait avec ta famille récemment ?

Section Six — Free-time Activities

Speaking Track 8 — Photo card — p.32

Intro: Parle-moi des photos.
1a) Quel est ton passe-temps préféré ?
1b) Est-ce que tu aimes aller à des concerts ? Pourquoi ? / pourquoi pas ?
1c) Parle-moi de ton film préféré.
1d) Quelle sorte de musique est-ce que tu aimes ?

Section Seven — Customs, Festivals and Celebrations

Speaking Track 9 — Role-play — p.36

Intro: Tu parles avec ton ami suisse. Moi, je suis ton ami.
1) Décris une fête ou une tradition de ton pays.
2) Qu'est-ce que tu fais normalement pour la célébrer ?
3) Quelle est ta fête ou ta tradition préférée ? Pourquoi ?
4) The student will now ask the teacher a question. The teacher should answer.
5) Qu'est-ce que tu as reçu pour ton dernier anniversaire ?

Section Eight — Celebrity Culture

Speaking Track 10 — Reading aloud — p.38

Intro: Lis-moi le texte.
1a) Qu'est-ce que tu penses de la presse ?
1b) Quel est le principal avantage de la vie d'une star ?
1c) Qui est ton héros ou ton héroïne ?
1d) Quels sont les inconvénients d'être célèbre ?

Theme 2 — Mixed Practice

Speaking Track 11 — Photo card — p.40

Intro: Parle-moi des photos.
1a) Quel est ton passe-temps préféré ? Pourquoi ?
1b) Est-ce que tu fais du sport ? Pourquoi / pourquoi pas ?
1c) Quelles activités sportives voudrais-tu essayer un jour ?
1d) Qu'est-ce que tu as fait le week-end dernier?

Speaking Track 12 — Reading aloud — p.41

Intro: Lis-moi le texte.
4a) Qu'est-ce que tu penses des célébrités ?
4b) Quelle est ton opinion sur les stars qui partagent des choses sur les réseaux sociaux ?
4c) Est-ce que tu as déjà rencontré une célébrité ?
4d) Parle-moi de ta star préférée.

Speaking Track 13 — Reading aloud — p.45
<u>Intro</u>: Lis-moi le texte.
6a) Quel est ton festival préféré ? Pourquoi ?
6b) Quelles sont les traditions de votre famille ?
6c) Qu'est-ce que tu aimes faire pour célébrer ton anniversaire ?
6d) Qu'est-ce que tu penses des fêtes ?

Speaking Track 14 — Role-play — p.48
<u>Intro</u>: Tu parles avec ton ami suisse. Moi, je suis ton ami.
1) Décris ton passe-temps préféré.
2) Quand est-ce que tu fais ce passe-temps ?
3) Quelle est l'activité que tu aimes le moins ? Pourquoi ?
4) The student will now ask the teacher a question. The teacher should answer.
5) Que fais-tu normalement avec tes copains ?

Section Nine — Travel and Tourism

Speaking Track 15 — Photo card — p.50
<u>Intro</u>: Parle-moi des photos.
1a) Est-ce que tu aimes utiliser les transports publics ? Pourquoi ? / pourquoi pas ?
1b) Parle-moi de tes dernières vacances.
1c) Est-ce que tu préfères les vacances en ville ou au bord de la mer ? Pourquoi ?
1d) Quel type de logement préfères-tu quand tu es en vacances ? Pourquoi ?

Section Eleven — Where People Live

Speaking Track 16 — Role-play — p.60
<u>Intro</u>: Tu parles avec ton ami québécois. Moi, je suis ton ami.
1) Décris ta ville ou ton village.
2) Où est-ce que tu aimes aller en ville ?
3) Qu'est-ce que tu penses de ta région ?
4) The student will now ask the teacher a question. The teacher should answer.
5) Quel temps fait-il dans ta région ?

Section Twelve — Environmental and Social Issues

Speaking Track 17 — Photo card — p.63
<u>Intro</u>: Parle-moi des photos.
4a) Quelle est ton opinion sur l'énergie verte ?
4b) Est-ce que tu penses que la pollution est un problème grave ?
4c) À ton avis, quelles activités humaines contribuent à la pollution ?
4d) Pourquoi certaines espèces sont-elles en train de disparaître ?

Theme 3 — Mixed Practice

Speaking Track 18 — Photo card — p.66
<u>Intro</u>: Parle-moi des photos.
2a) Comment est-ce que tu aides les autres ?
2b) À ton avis, est-ce que le réchauffement de la planète est une crise grave ? Pourquoi / pourquoi pas ?
2c) Comment est-ce qu'on peut protéger l'environnement ?
2d) Est-ce que tu penses que le chômage est un problème ? Pourquoi / pourquoi pas ?

Speaking Track 19 — Reading aloud — p.67
<u>Intro</u>: Lis-moi le texte.
4a) Qu'est-ce que tu penses des réseaux sociaux ?
4b) Quels sont les avantages d'Internet ?
4c) Comment est-ce que tu utilises la technologie ?
4d) Qu'est-ce que tu penses du streaming ?

Speaking Track 20 — Role-play — p.68
<u>Intro</u>: Tu parles avec ton amie française. Moi, je suis ton amie.
1) Où se trouve ta maison ou ton appartement ?
2) Quelle est ton opinion sur ta région ?
3) The student will now ask the teacher a question. The teacher should answer.
4) Pourquoi aimes-tu ta maison ou ton appartement ?
5) Qu'est-ce qu'on peut faire dans ta région ?

Speaking Track 21 — Reading aloud — p.75
<u>Intro</u>: Lis-moi le texte.
8a) Selon toi, quel est le plus grave problème dans le monde aujourd'hui ? Pourquoi ?
8b) Qu'est-ce qu'on peut faire pour lutter contre les attitudes racistes ?
8c) Comment réduire la pauvreté ?
8d) Est-ce que tu penses qu'il est important de voter ? Pourquoi ? / Pourquoi pas ?

Transcripts